On a Huge Hill

On a Huge Hill

A search for truth and integrity

Murray Dell

SCM PRESS LTD

*Unless otherwise indicated, biblical quotations
are taken from the Revised Standard Version*

0 334 02725 X

First published 1998
by SCM Press
9–17 St Albans Place, London N1 0NX

Typeset by Regent Typesetting, London
and printed and bound in Great Britain by
Biddles Ltd, Guildford and King's Lynn

On a huge hill,
Craggéd and steep, Truth stands, and he that will
Reach her, about must and about must go.

John Donne

For Ruth who shared sixteen years in Lyme Regis with me, and for our daughters Rebecca and Clare and son-in-law George, and for our unborn grandchild.

I wish to thank Molly and Fred, Joan, Ann and Maureen for their encouraging words after reading some or all of the typescript.

Preface

During sixteen years as Vicar of Lyme Regis I kept a diary (although someone more orderly would not have dreamt of calling it a diary). It was really just a collection of scribbled jottings on scraps of paper. After retiring, my first task was to put some of the jottings together and type them up. Two or three people have read the resultant typescript and said that it should be offered to a wider circle of readers.

The jottings are a record of my search for truth during the period of sixteen years in Lyme. No one, I hope, will think that I am offering a record of truth set in stone. The jottings are intended to be a record of a pursuit of truth, not an arrogant statement about the possession of truth. In order to reach truth I 'about must and about must go'. I am still going about and about on the huge hill.

I apologise in advance to any readers who might find my language sexist. It is not meant to be. Will the reader try to see the words 'son', 'him', 'hers' inclusively as 'son or daughter', 'him or her', 'his or hers'.

My thanks go to the town of Lyme Regis, to the Vicarage where I had my study and where I scribbled most of the jottings, to the people of Lyme Regis, and specially to the congregation of the Parish Church.

My family and I arrived in Lyme Regis in 1980 from Windhoek, Namibia. Lyme is called the Pearl of Dorset. It is a small, beautiful seaside town, proud of its beauty, proud of its history. It has always been a favourite with tourists, but its worldwide fame took a leap in 1980 when 'The French Lieutenant's Woman' was filmed there.

One of Lyme's ancient structures is the Parish Church. It stands not much more than a stone's throw from the sea, high above the beach, and from the churchyard wall one can see across Lyme Bay to Golden Cap and other parts of the lovely Dorset coast.

As I have said, these diary entries originated in my study as scribbled jottings on scraps of paper. When I came to type the jottings up, I took them out of any chronological order they might have had and rearranged them roughly in themes. The reader will, I hope, be able to perceive each theme – each train of thought – melting into the next.

An indication of Sources and Acknowledgments is given on pages 116–118.

Murray Dell

On a Huge Hill

I have often sought Truth on a huge hill, craggèd and steep – on Table Mountain, on the Drakensberg, on Blackford Hill, on Golden Cap – but since living in Lyme Regis I have usually sought her behind and below the Parish Church, on Church Beach.

I escape from the ecclesiastic, blue liassic confines of the church and go about and about, up the north path to the churchyard wall, then down to Long Entry, then further down to the beach below. From there, across the Bay, one can see Golden Cap, and much besides.

It has always been like that. My present escapes to Church Beach have followed the pattern of other escapes, such as the one from the clergy retreat in Natal.

I had only recently been ordained, and this now was my first clergy retreat. It was taking place at a public school in the midst of Natal's rolling hills. All around was an abundance of beauty: huge hills, green fields, flowers, birds, endless sunshine.

Contrasting with the Eden-like setting, the actual retreat seemed to be enclosed, introverted, claustrophobic.

I

God was being reduced to fit into the jargon used by the retreat conductor, into the dogma he was expounding, into the black cassocks we were wearing. The whole package was esoteric, desiccated, macabre.

At coffee-time on the second day, as we were all emerging from the chapel in our long, silent, black line, I looked to see what sort of expression my best friend had on his face. I saw that he looked as pained as I was feeling, so we made contact with each other, hatched a plan, went to our rooms, threw off our cassocks, and went walking.

We walked and we walked. We walked all over the verdant hills and fields, revelling in the beauty we saw and in the people and wild life we encountered.

It was an exhilarating, liberating experience. We discovered that God is greater and more ubiquitous than the God of the jargon and dogma and cassocks.

The memory has remained with me all these years, and has led me to beware of limiting the size of the canvas on which we paint the picture of the face and activity of God.

Even before the retreat in Natal, there was the retreat at my theological college. At the time I was sheriff (senior student) and should therefore have set a good example to my fellow-students, but sometimes ecclesiaphobia becomes impossible to bear, and I broke out and led a minor rebellion.

The conductor of the retreat had been rabbiting on in the chapel about ecclesiastical matters and high-flown doctrine, and it had all become nauseating to me, and eventually I had to escape.

It was clear to me that three or four other students were also suffering; therefore, having decided as covertly as possible on a plan of action, we climbed the stairs to my room and had a party. It was just a relatively innocent party of tea and biscuits, during which we had to be as quiet as possible and not deprive other students of their retreat silence. For more than an hour, however, we were able to let off steam.

Afterwards, I expected to be reprimanded by my Principal, perhaps even stripped of my sheriff's badge, but evidently he hadn't heard about the party or, wise man that he was, he realized that the content of the retreat was not the sort of fare to serve up to theological students in the mid-1960s.

Today I was on Church Beach early in the morning, before the early service.

I stood at the water's edge and watched the dawn arrive in a trinity of light. At first the sun was a burning bush, small and red, over Golden Cap, then slowly it became larger and yellow and dazzling, embracing me with its burgeoning warmth. Gradually everything became illumined: myself, the cliffs, the beach I was standing on, its sand and pebbles and rocks. And the reflection of the sun came across the water to where I was standing, and touched me.

Always I seem to be searching for truth, and invariably come to realize, in the midst of the search, that it is not so much a question of finding as of being found.

> I sought the Lord, and afterward I knew
> He moved my soul to seek Him, seeking me;
> It was not I that found, O Saviour true –
> No, I was found of Thee.
>
> Thou didst reach forth Thy hand and mine enfold;
> I walked and sank not on the storm-vexed sea.
> 'Twas not so much that I on Thee took hold,
> As Thou, dear Lord, on me.
>
> I find, I walk, I love, but O the whole
> Of love is but my answer, Lord, to Thee;
> For Thou wast long beforehand with my soul,
> Alway Thou lovedst me.
>
> Author unknown

ॐ

> As he walked by the Sea of Galilee, he saw two brothers, Simon who is called Peter and Andrew his brother, casting a net into the sea; for they were fishermen. And he said to them, 'Follow me . . .'
>
> (Matt. 4.18–19)

Twenty centuries later the call can still reach us. The words 'Follow me' can escape from the confines of the page, the ink, the Bible and become present to us.

On Church Beach I hear that call. It is a primal call that comes to me as surely as each wave rolls on to the beach,

4

as surely as the sun's reflection comes to me across the water, and I hear it at the centre of my being.

∾

He comes to us as One unknown, without a name, as of old, by the lake-side, He came to those men who knew Him not. He speaks to us the same word: 'Follow thou me!' and sets us to the tasks which He has to fulfil for our time. He commands. And to those who obey Him, whether they be wise or simple, He will reveal Himself in the toils, the conflicts, the sufferings which they shall pass through in His fellowship, and, as an ineffable mystery, they shall learn in their own experience Who He is.

Albert Schweitzer

∾

Albert Schweitzer wrote those words at the beginning of the twentieth century.

'He *comes*,' he wrote, not 'He came.' 'He *comes to us*,' he wrote, not 'He came to them.'

He comes to us, to Schweitzer and others, at the beginning of the twentieth century. He comes to us at the end of the twentieth century.

Jesus of Nazareth didn't just say to Simon Peter and Andrew, while walking by the sea of Galilee, 'Follow me.' He says the same to us, as we stand on a beach or sit on a huge hill or walk meditatively in Oxford Street.

He didn't just take children in his arms and bless them,

while sitting with his followers in Judaea. He does the same for us, if we will let him.

What happened to them then can be *remembered* by us now, internalized by us now, apprehended by us now. The past can be made present, and active, full of power.

❧

That is equally, or specially, true of the eucharist.

As the words and actions of the eucharist unfold, it is as though the walls of the sanctuary – the sanctuary in which we are kneeling – fall away, and we are kneeling not at a communion rail but in an upper room or on a Judaean hill or by a Galilean lake.

What was available to those men and women years ago and miles away becomes available to us.

The hem of his robe is brought within an arm's length, and we have only to reach out to touch it. The grace is waiting to flow into us.

❧

I saw the morn break glorious o'er the sea
With all the ritual of its pageantry:
Soft herald lights shone first, then splendidly
Crimson and gold gave welcome royally:
The dim dawn curtains parted, and the sun,
A great gold circle, slowly, solemnly,
Proclaiming that a new day had begun,
Rose from his palace underneath the sea.

From that magnificence I went my way
Down to the village church below the hill,

And there with simple souls I knelt to pray,
With them to learn submission to His will
Who with true poverty could be content;
And, as my Lord in mercy came to me
In the small circle of the Sacrament,
I marvelled at His deep humility.

Father Andrew

∾

And, as my Lord in mercy came to me
In the small circle of the Sacrament,
I marvelled at His deep humility.

The church has in its hands the most powerful therapeutic tool in existence, namely the grace which lies at the heart of the eucharist and which is alive with possibilities for the deep healing of the inner self. In the eucharist the communicant can find welcome, judgment, understanding, mercy, forgiveness, reassurance, acceptance, validation . . .

I am a priest of the process, an enabler, a facilitator. I should like to make the grace more available to the communicant, and I rage against the inconsistencies and irrelevancies and verbosities under which the grace is smothered.

∾

Jesus, when He called His disciples, required from them nothing beyond the will to follow Him.

Albert Schweitzer

Albert Schweitzer, having made an offer to the Paris Missionary Society to serve its mission-field in West Africa, became embroiled in a dispute as to whether his beliefs were sufficiently orthodox. On the one hand were people who were loath to lose the opportunity of acquiring the mission doctor for whom they had so ardently longed; on the other hand the strictly orthodox objected. It was resolved to invite Schweitzer to appear before the Society's committee for an examination into his beliefs. Schweitzer would not agree to this. He based his refusal on the fact that Jesus, when he called his disciples, required from them nothing beyond the will to follow him.

❧

This year I found the Christmas services quite embarrassing. In the midst of reciting some of the extravagant language about Jesus of Nazareth I found myself wondering what picture of Jesus I was giving to people, what I was expecting them to believe.

The carols and the readings and the creed were telling us about the child being the only-begotten Son of God, the King of Angels, Word of the Father, Christ, the Messiah, a holy Child, very God of very God, born of a pure Virgin, and more besides. What were people making of it?

I am sure that many churchgoers are happy with such language: they have grown up with it and have no problem with it. But what about others, who must surely find it impossible to take on board the complete and instant package of belief that we seem to expect of them?

I should like to encourage people to start not with the divinity of Jesus but with his humanity.

There is a thread running through the Gospels which gives us a picture of a human Jesus of Nazareth: a Jesus born into an ordinary family, a man of his time who shared many of the beliefs of the people of his time, who shared the poverty of ordinary people, who wandered through a small region of the Middle East relating to people, telling them stories, teaching them a demanding ethic of love, imparting to them a gift of understanding, helping them to find meaning and purpose.

To start at the very beginning – what an experiment that would be! I feel compelled to join such an experiment myself. In other words, instead of having the extravagant language about Jesus' divinity set before us, could we not try to see a more human Jesus of Nazareth and begin to follow the man? Then, in the course of our following, we may well discover more and more about him. In Schweitzer's words, we may learn in our 'own experience Who He is'.

Today I listened to a thirty-minute sermon on faith. Faith this, faith that, have faith and you will achieve this, have faith and such-and-such will become possible for you. Faith, faith, faith. It was an erudite, model sermon delivered by a spick-and-span minister who should go far.

So why did I find myself wriggling, uncomfortable,

wanting to escape? Was it only because the sermon left me aware of how poor and small my miserable little bit of faith is? Or was there something wrong somewhere? Was there an exaltation of faith which there shouldn't have been? Was faith being placed on a pedestal where she shouldn't be? The preacher didn't actually say this, but because of the way in which he emphasized faith he was virtually saying that our salvation is achieved by our faith.

No, no, no. Important as faith is, faith has to play second fiddle to grace. We are saved not by faith but by grace.

For by grace you have been saved through faith; and this is not your own doing, it is the gift of God.

(Eph. 2.8)

☙

It's no good as a preacher exhorting one's congregation never-endingly to have faith, to have more faith: to have more faith and then they will be delivered from this, to have more faith and then they will be delivered from that. The have-more-faith approach can be the downhill road to despair and guilt, and many there are who are led that way.

Much more important than having one's faith whipped up – which can be a fairly superficial operation – is being helped to recognize, perhaps ten leagues beneath the surface of one's personality, one's need of grace.

☙

The man of faith considers his faith, even his faith, to be a blessing, a gift, something he is given, something that comes to him, something he receives, something to be thankful for. He can't see it coming from himself, from his emptiness and weakness and nakedness. He feels that it is part of the fountain of God flowing within him.

> *And a woman who had had a flow of blood for twelve years and could not be healed by any one, came up behind him, and touched the fringe of his garment; and immediately her flow of blood ceased. Jesus said, 'Someone touched me; for I perceive that power has gone forth from me.'*   (Luke 8.43–48)

In Rembrandt's drawing 'Christ and the Ailing Woman' the woman is shown as a pale figure approaching Jesus. She is distracted, ill, yet now single-mindedly but weakly she is approaching Jesus from behind to reach out and touch the fringe of his garment.

Her reaching out and touching is her faith. But salvation is not brought to her by her faith; it is brought to her by the power going forth from Jesus, by his grace.

His grace is apprehended by her faith.

Grace and faith can meet not only in the ailing woman, not only in the pages of the Bible, not only in the past, but in the present, in the human being in the present moment.

In heart and mind we can go even unto Galilee; Galilee can come even unto us. Grace and faith can meet here and now, as they did there and then. Each meeting of his grace and our faith advances our wholeness by another degree.

We don't have to reach out very far.

This morning, again at dawn, I was on Church Beach, standing at the water's edge and watching the sun rise. A brilliant orange rim appeared above the horizon, then the whole orange ball revealed itself, and as it did so it cast an orange strip of reflection towards me across the sea. I strolled along the beach, and still the reflection, the orange now yellower, came to me. I walked ten yards further, and still the reflection came to me. I walked another hundred yards along the water's edge, and still the reflection, now very yellow and much brighter, came to me. Wherever I stood at the water's edge, the reflection was at my feet.

One gets in touch not by reaching out through miles and years, but by apprehending what is at one's very feet.

I have always been grateful to Professor G.W.H. Lampe for a sentence in one of his books:

> *Grace is the biblical word used to denote just that attitude of free and undeserved love in which Jesus approached Zacchaeus and the father in the parable received the erring son.*

Grace is a gem with many facets. In Jesus' encounter with Zacchaeus and in the parable of the erring son (Luke 19.1f. and 15.11f.) the facets of grace are, among others, yearning, tenderness, judgment, understanding, acceptance. By grace, apprehended by faith, Zacchaeus and the erring son become something of what they are meant to be.

In his encounter with Zacchaeus, Jesus saw beyond the corrupt quisling to the infinite possibilities within the man. In the parable, the father saw not so much an erring prodigal as his beloved son.

∾

We tend too often and too much to denigrate human beings as miserable offenders, and having been denigrated they will perhaps tend to behave how they have been perceived.

A contrary view of human beings is expressed in a scene from Franco Zeffirelli's film *Brother Sun, Sister Moon*, the story of a few years in the life of St Francis of Assisi.

Francis and his first followers walk from Assisi to Rome to ask the Pope to bless their new little movement. Barefoot, dishevelled, dressed in ragged habits, they are ushered in to the Vatican's sumptuousness to be confronted by Pope Innocent III sitting magnificently on his throne. Hesitantly Francis begins to speak his simple gospel words, saying that he and his followers wish to live simply according to the teachings of their Lord, and the Pope, despite his sumptuousness and sophistication and power and guile, is deeply moved by the men's poverty and simplicity and humility, by his recognition that they are fearfully and wonderfully made. He gets up off his throne and goes to the little band of men and says, 'In our obsession with original sin, we too often forget original innocence.'

∾

'Vicar, why do you go on believing as you do in human potential, when there is so much evidence all round us to the contrary?', a parishioner asked me this morning.

My reply: 'Because of what I see shining in the lives of twelve men in the year 1209.'

St Francis of Assisi was joined by Bernard, then by Peter, and soon there were twelve of them: Francis and eleven others. It is in the early life together of those twelve men that we see the most perfect expression of Christian discipleship.

They went to Rome to tell the Pope about their new life, then they returned north to live out that life. This they did in a hut. Near Assisi they found a small abandoned hut which for some months became the setting for the most idyllic days of the Franciscan movement. It was there that twelve human beings showed what human beings have it in them to be. Bound together by love and joy and peace they lived out a life of poverty and simplicity and humility in an attempt to express their devotion to Jesus of Nazareth.

Eventually a man and his donkey brought the idyll to an end. The man appeared at the door of the hut, talking to his donkey. 'At last,' he said to the donkey, 'we've found a place to live,' and he pushed the donkey into the hut.

Francis, true to his love of humility, said to his eleven companions that it was perhaps time to move on. So they left the hut, letting the man and his donkey have it.

∽

If I were to visit Cain in prison – Cain, who has murdered his brother Abel and is now in prison – I'd want to try to see in him not just a murderer but something else. I'd want to try to make contact with a different Cain from the Cain who has been tried in court and reviled in the media. Surely, I'd think, there must be something good about Cain for me to make contact with, some potential, some inner endowment, some part of him that his Mum knows and loves, some glowing ember which he himself may never have recognized. I'd want to try to fan that ember into a flame, in the hope that the fire would spread and consume Cain's murderous bent.

That may be the way in which I did my prison visiting in Windhoek. The prisoners weren't murderers: the ones I ministered to were rascals, but delightful rascals, and I got on well with them. My prison visiting wasn't what the secular world would call a success; in fact I had my permit to visit the prison withdrawn. It was the tough apartheid era and I can only assume that the authorities did not approve of my trying to see in the prisoners something that they themselves were perhaps not seeing. I often wonder about two men in particular: whether my (and my family's) relationship with them made a difference to their future lives.

James Aggrey tells a story called 'The Eagle That Would Not Fly'.

A man caught a young eagle and took it home. He put it among his hens and ducks and turkeys, and he gave it chicken food to eat.

15

Five years later a naturalist visited the man, and when he saw the eagle he said 'That bird is an eagle, not a chicken.'

'I know,' said the man, 'but I have trained it to be a chicken. It is no longer an eagle, even though its wingspan is fifteen feet.'

'No,' said the naturalist, 'it is an eagle still. It has the heart of an eagle, and I will make it soar high up to the heavens.'

'No,' said the owner, 'it is now a chicken, and it will never fly.'

They agreed to test it.

The naturalist picked up the eagle, held it high and said with great intensity, 'Eagle, you are an eagle; you belong to the sky and not to this earth. Stretch out your wings and fly.'

The eagle turned this way and that, and then, looking down, saw the chickens eating their food, and jumped down.

'There you are,' said the owner, 'I told you it was a chicken.'

'No,' said the naturalist, 'it is an eagle. It has always had the heart of an eagle. Give it another chance tomorrow.'

So the next day the naturalist took the eagle to the roof of the house, held it up and said, 'Eagle, you are an eagle, stretch out your wings and fly.'

But when the eagle saw the hens and ducks and turkeys running round the yard, it jumped down and joined in.

'There,' said the owner again, 'I told you it was a chicken.'

'No,' said the naturalist again, 'it is still an eagle, and it still has the heart of an eagle. Just give it one more chance. It will fly tomorrow.'

The next morning the naturalist got up very early. He took the eagle out of the city, away from the houses, to the foot of a high mountain. The sun was just rising, the mountain was tipped with gold, and every boulder sparkled. It was a beautiful morning.

The naturalist picked up the eagle and said to it, 'Eagle, you are an eagle. You belong to the sky and not to this earth; stretch out your wings and fly.'

The eagle looked around and trembled as if new life were coming to it – but it did not fly.

The naturalist then made the eagle look straight at the sun.

Suddenly the eagle stretched out its wings and, with the screech of an eagle, it flew higher and higher and never returned.

∽

I am bothered by the thought that for much of my professional life I have been conniving with people in their belief that it is OK for them to live as hens and ducks and turkeys; not challenging them sufficiently to fly, to recognize that they are eagles, to become what they are, to discover and live out what they are, to live out the glorious liberty of the children of God. I am bothered by the thought that not only have I encouraged other people to live as hens and ducks and turkeys but that I have tended to live that way myself.

∽

There are three tame ducks in our back yard
Dabbling in mud and trying hard
To get their share and maybe more
Of the overflowing barnyard store,
Satisfied with the task they're at
Of eating and sleeping and getting fat.
But whenever the free wild ducks go by
In a long line streaming down the sky,
They cock a quizzical, puzzled eye
And flap their wings and try to fly.

I think my soul is a tame old duck
Dabbling around in barnyard muck,
Fat and lazy, with useless wings.
But sometimes when the North wind sings
And wild ones hurtle overhead,
It remembers something lost and dead,
And cocks a wary, bewildered eye,
And makes a feeble attempt to fly.
It's fairly content with the state it's in,
But it isn't the duck it might have been.

Kenneth Kaufman

It bothers me to think that in my career as curate and dean and vicar I have done so much to encourage people to think of themselves as tame ducks whose horizons are restricted to being

> *Satisfied with the task they're at*
> *Of eating and sleeping and getting fat*

rather than to think of themselves as free wild ducks. It bothers me to think that that too, by and large, is how I have thought of myself.

In so many respects we have lived bourgeois lives, enslaved, in one way or another, by religion. We, a Christian nation, are a nation of barnyard ducks. There should be a convincing summons to us to live true, to live as free wild ducks streaming down the sky, to live out the glorious liberty of the children of God.

∾

When one reads the poetry of the First World War one is frequently surprised by descriptions of nature appearing alongside descriptions of war. One would have thought that the natural world – certainly any perception of it – would have been obliterated by the mud and blood of the trenches; but no, the beauty of the natural world still breaks through. Thus

> *The magpies in Picardy*
> *Are more than I can tell.*
> *They flicker down the dusty roads*
> *And cast a magic spell*
> *On the men who march through Picardy,*
> *Through Picardy to hell.*

And

> *In Flanders fields the poppies blow*
> *Between the crosses, row on row*
> *That mark our place; and in the sky*
> *The larks, still bravely singing, fly*
> *Scarce heard amid the guns below.*

And

Sombre the night is.
And though we have our lives, we know
What sinister threat lurks there . . .
But hark! joy – joy – strange joy.
Lo! heights of night ringing with unseen larks.
Music showering our upturned list'ning faces . . .

In the midst of a most grim reality, another reality breaks through: a higher reality, an unchanging reality, an ultimate reality, an eternal reality, a joyful reality.

We, living for the most part our humdrum, second rate, sometimes sordid lives, must learn the art of upturning our listening faces to perceive that higher reality.

It comes to us as surprise, as blessing, as mercy, as gift, as a gift to be apprehended.

❧

Francis was rebuilding old churches near Assisi, churches that had fallen into disrepair, and he needed money to buy the necessary building materials.

His father, a cloth merchant, wasn't short of a penny or two, so Francis sold some of his father's cloth to raise money to buy what he needed.

His father, Peter Bernadone, was so angry that he made Francis appear before the Bishop of Assisi at a kind of Bishop's Court, and Francis was charged with helping himself to his father's goods.

In a typically dramatic, theatrical gesture, Francis took off his clothes saying 'Right, I'll give back to my father the money I owe him, and I also give back to him these clothes he provided me with.' Then to the crowd that had gathered he said, 'Up until now I have called Peter Bernadone my father, but now I wish to say not "my father, Peter Bernadone" but "Our Father, which art in heaven".'

If for Francis God was Father, then Francis was a son, a son of God. And that is what we all are, whether we know it or not: sons and daughters of God. That is our status, that is our identity, that is who we are, that is our place in the universe.

It is a discovery to be made: discovering what it means to be a human being, what it means to be fully human.

Discovering your sonship or daughtership can be like climbing a mountain. You have the world spread out below you, clear and beautiful, and afterwards, when you have descended to the plain, you still belong to the mountain and have a higher perspective on life.

It can be like hang-gliding. In the air you experience lightness and freedom, and afterwards, when you are back on the ground, you know you will never again be fully an earthling.

It can be like swimming with dolphins. During the swim you become attuned to the heartbeat of the universe, and afterwards, when you have emerged from the water, you will always be something of an alien in your former existence.

You emerge with the ethos, the perspective, the righteousness of your experience clinging to you.

There is nothing you have to do to achieve your sonship or daughtership. There is nothing you can do except discover it, recognize it.

Let it be so. You are a son or daughter of God, as the erring prodigal was a son in the embrace of his father. Let it be so for you. No effort is required. It is something you are given. Receive it. Receive it by faith. Receive it by faith with thanksgiving.

After Zacchaeus had been accepted by Jesus of Nazareth and after the erring prodigal had been embraced by his father, they were not necessarily any gooder, any better, morally speaking, than they had been before, but their lives had now been turned round. Zacchaeus the outcast now had a friend, and the prodigal now was a son on his father's estate. To both of them a new life had opened up, and both now had a vision of a life to grow into.

It's a little like the love of a woman for an alcoholic husband. Their friends see only the love of a woman for a drunk: they see in him no goodness, no virtue, no righteousness. But his wife loves him and sees something very different in him, even a beauty. His beauty is in the eye of the beholder, his wife. If he has any sense he will respond to how his wife sees him, and he will spend the rest of his life becoming how his wife sees him, growing into the beauty seen by his wife.

It was the only thing he had. Love. And that's what he gave me. He shared it with me. Sat at my table and ate my food and gave me love.

Zacchaeus, interviewed in *The Davidson Affair*

What Jesus of Nazareth gave to Simon Peter, Andrew, James, John, Zacchaeus, Mary Magdalene, Mary, Martha, and to all others who were willing to receive it, was love.

As we *remember* him, that is what we are given. The past becomes present, and what was given to them then is given to us now.

What we see in Jesus tells us more about the heart of the universe than anything else . . . However it may look on the surface, reality at bottom is like that: love of that quality is the most real, the most powerful, thing in the world . . . In Jesus Christ we have a window through into ultimate reality itself, into God . . . Jesus of Nazareth is the deepest probe into the meaning of things that we have been given. For in him we reach rock-bottom – that rock of love on which the whole universe is constructed. What we see on the surface of history in Jesus is what it's like at the centre. That's what, in traditional language, is meant by the 'divinity' of Christ.

John A.T. Robinson

'Only when I was singing did I feel loved,' said Maria Callas of her childhood. That feeling, I am sure, is echoed by countless numbers of other people. 'Only when I was clean did I feel loved' or 'Only when I was good did I feel loved'. The psyches of people are littered, polluted with the conditionality of the love they received as children. The condition may not be spoken, but it is there, implicit and dark and menacing, in the way the parent relates to the child.

The love of Jesus of Nazareth is different. People are not told 'You've got to deserve it, you've got to earn it, you've got to be worthy of my acceptance.' His love is given unconditionally, as a gift.

Such love can emanate from parents. As a young man grows up, he may stumble for this reason or that, he may fall over this or that obstacle, he may feel judgment and discipline reaching him from his father, but all the time he knows that his father loves him. He feels his father embracing him and saying 'I love you. I love you not because you are perfect. You're not. I love you because you are my son.'

∾

A mother who lives in the next town had a son who was caught up in the teenage drugs scene. Eventually he left home. He cut himself off from her in every way, except that he let her know where he was.

Every week she posted a postcard to him which said 'I love you, I'll love you always.' Unconditional love. Not 'I'll love you if and when you give up drugs' but 'I love you, I'll love you always.'

After many months the son appeared on his mother's doorstep saying 'Hi, Mom, I've been a silly ass, haven't I?' She said simply 'Yes, you have been, but now let's let the past be past,' and she welcomed him in.

Love given away. A difficult thing for people to understand when all their lives they have laboured under the burdensome thinking that love has to be bought. Godly love is grace love, love given free.

May your roots go down deep into the soil of God's marvelous love; and may you be able to feel and understand, as all God's children should, how long, how wide, how deep, and how high his love really is; and to experience this love for yourselves, though it is so great that you will never see the end of it or fully know or understand it. And so at last you will be filled up with God himself.

(Eph. 3.17b–19 – The Living Bible)

Love bade me welcome: yet my soul drew back,
Guiltie of dust and sinne.
But quick-ey'd Love, observing me grow slack
From my first entrance in,
Drew nearer to me, sweetly questioning
If I lack'd any thing.

'A guest,' I answer'd, 'worthy to be here':
Love said, 'You shall be he.'
'I the unkinde, ungratefull? Ah, my deare,
I cannot look on thee.'
Love took my hand, and smiling did reply,
'Who made the eyes but I?'

'Truth Lord, but I have marr'd them: let my shame
Go where it doth deserve.'
'And know you not,' sayes Love, 'who bore the
blame?'
'My deare, then I will serve.'
'You must sit down,' sayes Love, 'and taste my meat':
So I did sit and eat.

George Herbert (1593–1633)

∾

Jesus was a person-centred rabbi. He didn't love religion so much that he felt he had to pour the person into the mould of religion. He loved the person so much that what he wanted for him was his (the person's) highest good.

We so often make the mistake of loving this society so much or that church so much or some particular brand of morality so much that when we try to help someone we feel we have to fit him into the society or the church or the brand of morality, and that may not be what is best for him.

❧

Love is powerless in the sense in which we usually think of power, in the sense of having power over the other person, in the sense of foisting on him allegiance to this religion or that morality or that institution. Love leaves the other person free, leaves his future free to unfold in a way that is right for him.

In the parable, there is nothing strong-armed about the father's embrace of the prodigal son, nothing possessive about it, nothing manipulative about it, nothing compelling about it. The boy is left free to be embraced or not to be embraced. It is love on offer, on offer to be received or rejected. The power of the father is nil in the sense in which we usually think of power. But it is a true saving, reconciling, redeeming power.

❧

Today R. related a story about a boy who ran away from home to the other side of the world, and he stayed away, and he didn't write home, and the years rolled on, and eventually ten or fifteen years had passed and he still hadn't been in touch with his mother.

Then he travelled back to his home town. He got a bed with an old school friend, and he wondered what he could do, whether he could ever go back to his mother's house, how he could make contact with his mother.

After a few days he wrote a letter to his mother: 'I don't know whether you ever want to see me again after the way I've treated you, but I'm here back in town, and if you want me to come and see you, then please tomorrow afternoon hang a sheet on the washing line.'

The following afternoon, with great trepidation, he walked round to the back of his mother's house where he knew he'd be able to see the washing line. His heart skipped a beat, for there wasn't just one sheet on it – the whole washing line was full of sheets. All the sheets the mother had in the house were flapping in the breeze.

In the love, in the powerlessness of love, in the helplessness of love, there is great pain. The greater the love, the more ubiquitous the love, the greater the pain, the greater the suffering.

In May 1373 Julian of Norwich had a series of visions about the love of God. She was ill, and was expected to die of the illness. The Hundred Years' War was raging in Europe. And Europe was mourning its 25 million Black Death victims. Despite all, she was able to write a paeon of praise to the love of God.

> *Our Lord showed me spiritually how intimately he loves us. I saw that he is everything that we know to be good and helpful. In his love he clothes us, enfolds and embraces us; that tender love completely surrounds us, never to leave us . . .*

'You will not be overcome' was said very distinctly and firmly to give us confidence and comfort for whatever troubles may come. (Our Lord) did not say, 'You will never have a rough passage, you will never be over-strained, you will never feel uncomfortable,' but he did say, 'You will never be overcome.' God wants us to pay attention to these words, so as to trust him always with strong confidence, through thick and thin. For he loves us . . .

∾

I am sure that neither death, nor life, nor angels, nor principalities, nor things present, nor things to come, nor powers, nor height, nor depth, nor anything else in all creation, will be able to separate us from the love of God in Christ Jesus our Lord.

(Rom.8.38f.)

∾

The love of God in Christ is poured into the eucharist, therefore that is what we receive when we go up to the communion rail to receive the bread and the wine.

I do not feel committed to the sacramental words of administration 'The body of Christ' and 'The blood of Christ'. For the sake of people who believe that the words smack too much of literalism or even cannibalism, I'd be happy to administer the bread and the wine with some such words as 'The love of God' or 'The grace of our Lord Jesus Christ' or simply 'God loves you'.

The eucharist is a sacrament of unconditional love given and received – at least that is what it is surely meant to be. But we stipulate that in order to receive unconditional love people first have to be baptized, they first have to be confirmed, they first have to be able to stand up in church and say the creed. That is inconsistent with the unconditionality of the love offered to all and sundry by Jesus of Nazareth.

~

In Mrs Alexander's well-loved hymn, we sing about the dear Lord

Who died to save us all.

That, however, is not the most important line of the hymn. The most important line is

O dearly, dearly has he loved.

The saving was done not by his death but by his dear, dear love. He loved so dearly that he loved to the end, to the death.

Often in Christian preaching, the death of Jesus of Nazareth appears to become separated off from his life, so that his death on the cross is somehow treated as something separate from his life. But they are not separate. His death was the culmination, the ultimate expression of his life; and his life was a life of love, and it is his life, his love that does the saving.

It is not the death of soldiers that achieves victory in war but what lies behind their death, namely the soldiers themselves, their patriotism, their duty, their courage, their endurance.

It is not the laying down of the shepherd's life that ensures the safety of his sheep but the shepherd himself, the quality of his care for the sheep that may eventuate in his laying down his life for them.

The saving is done not by a death but by a person, by his love.

It is not the cross that saves. What saves is the man behind the cross, and the love of that man.

☙

The love is given, to be received. It is only efficacious if it is received. Therefore the learning of the art of receiving is of paramount importance.

☙

In a speech he made to the elders of Ephesus St Paul quotes Jesus as having said 'It is more blessed to give than to receive.'

I'd want to say this to St Paul: 'Paul,' I'd say, 'there's no sign of such a saying in the Gospels, and to me it doesn't sound like an authentic saying of Jesus. I think you're having us on. I think you've got it wrong. I think you're passing on to us a non-saying of Jesus.'

The non-saying of Jesus has had a profound effect on Christianity because it is the wisdom that conventional institutional Christianity has tended to embody: that it is more blessed to give than to receive.

For years I went along with such wisdom until I came to see how desiccated it was, how dried up it was making the people who subscribed to it, myself included. For years I took it as gospel truth and proclaimed it. Was I not a preacher, and did I not have an obligation to set before people the Christian ethic, and was not the Christian ethic to give, and give, and give even more?

I took too long, fool that I was, to realize that I was trying to get water out of a stone: that people cannot give – that people cannot give very much – until they have begun to learn how to receive. It was a turning upside down of my stupid, conventional, institutional wisdom. What a dimwit I'd been!

∽

This Christmas I have heard a commercial jingle on television. It goes something like this:

> Christmas, Christmas, Christmas time
> Is giving, giving, giving time.

Is it? I'm not sure it is. I think I'd prefer the jingle, if we have to have jingles, to go like this:

> Christmas, Christmas, Christmas time
> Is receiving, receiving, receiving time.

My version of it doesn't scan quite as well, but I'd want to defend it as embodying the meaning of Christmas a little better.

By receiving I don't mean any sort of acquisitive, materialistic taking or grasping or getting, like being proud because one has received three bottles of wine or four boxes of peppermint creams for Christmas. I mean taking seriously the words of the Christmas Gospel:

But as many as received him, to them gave
he power to become the sons of God.

As we *remember* Jesus of Nazareth at Christmas time the
past can become present for us, and active, and full of
power, and the words 'But as many as received him, to
them gave he power to become the sons of God' can
become for us 'But as many as *receive* him, to them *gives*
he power to become the sons of God.'

At Christmas time it is first and foremost a matter of
receiving him.

ॐ

That is especially true in the eucharist. Week by week the
doing of the eucharist can become an exercise in receiving
Jesus of Nazareth. As we kneel at the communion rail we
receive him, and the 'Amen' we say is a profound 'Thank
you' welling up from within us.

Having received him, we possess the impetus to give.

ॐ

If we are to receive in that kind of way, then we need to
know how to be still, how to be quiet, how to be expec-
tant, how to be receptive.

There is a need for outer silence before the eucharist,
and a need for inner silence throughout the eucharist. And
when I stand at the top of a hill or on a quiet beach I
inwardly rage against my companions if they begin to
chatter.

ॐ

Receiving can be a hard lesson for self-reliant, self-sufficient, independent people to learn – people who are used to paying every inch of their way, people who have not been brought up on the philosophy of grace, people who have not been brought up on the philosophy of generous hospitality received and given. One then has to break out of the grip of conventional wisdom, out of the grip of one's stiff-upper-lip upbringing, almost out of the grip of one's personality.

Perhaps need is the spur, and one only learns to receive if one has a sense of need, a sense of inner need: a sense of poverty, a sense of blindness, a sense of nakedness.

∾

Receiving is incomplete in itself, just as giving is incomplete in itself. Part of the dynamics of discipleship is an oscillation between receiving and giving: receiving and giving, receiving and giving throughout life.

∾

Someone who was a learner in the kingdom of God was J. Hers was one of the most emotionally difficult funerals I have ever had to take, because she had brought a whiff of the kingdom of God to the town, then suddenly she was no more.

Many people, or most people, and not a few church-people among them, feel that they have to be strong, powerful, tough. J. showed us how to be great by being weak, powerless, vulnerable. Although she was a highly-cultured and capable person she saw herself as weak and powerless and vulnerable, and she helped me to understand the upside down values of the kingdom of God, she helped me to see how the last can be first.

> Blessed are the last: in the kingdom of God
> they are first.
> Blessed are those who believe themselves to
> be flawed: in the kingdom of God they are
> flawless.
> Blessed are those who are weak: they shall be
> filled with the strength of God.
> Blessed are those who are powerless: they shall
> possess the power of God.
> Blessed are those who are vulnerable: in the
> kingdom of God they are invulnerable.
> Blessed are the humble: for they shall be
> exalted.

J. took the wealth of her personality out of the church and into the town where she was a servant among us, a servant of people and plants and animals. Her favourite animals? The ducks on the river. And hedgehogs. Once she called out the fire brigade to rescue a hedgehog trapped in an inaccessible spot. And donkeys, who were her perfect companions in their gentleness and humility and peace.

Unintentionally she taught us a lesson at almost every turn. She taught us about the place of possessions in life. Who else could have laughed at herself, as she did, when suddenly remembering in Broad Street that she had left her windows open and her doors unlocked, and the proceeds from her Plant Sale lying in her sitting room?

Suddenly she wasn't so capable. Arthritic knees, operations, and confined to the house. Now she showed the completeness of her personality, because now she was not just the giver, the servant: cheerfully she now received from others, she allowed others to serve her. Had the giver known this all her life, or was she only now learning it: the importance of knowing not just how to give but how to receive?

I suppose she was childlike. Not childish but childlike. She was humble, she was filled with wonder, she had that childlike capacity to receive.

> *Jesus said, 'Truly, I say to you, unless you turn and become like children, you will never enter the kingdom of heaven.'* (Matt. 18.3)

ல

We must never forget to be thankful for what we receive.

> *There's magic in thanksgiving. You may begin with a cup of coffee, but once you start, the gratefulness swells and the causes multiply. Finally, it seems the more you thank the more you have, and the more you get to be thankful for – and, of course, that's the whole spiritual keystone.*

> Fulton Oursler

ல

The ultimate receiving to be done is the receiving into ourselves of holy spirit, the spiritual energy that empowered Jesus of Nazareth. It is no wonder that I say that the cultivation of the art of receiving is of paramount and primary importance.

∽

In speaking of receiving holy spirit into ourselves I am not sure that I am saying anything very different from what I mean when I speak of Zacchaeus receiving the grace of Jesus of Nazareth or the prodigal son receiving the love of his father. They are simply different ways of speaking about our apprehension of God.

It is only when we are at the end of our own resources that holy spirit can find space within us. The grace of Jesus of Nazareth can only penetrate into us through cracks in our facade. The love of the Father can only get in by soaking into our felt need of love.

∽

When I was a young, green curate I always found the approach of Trinity Sunday a daunting prospect. The idea of the Trinity was so incredibly difficult, so intellectual, so cerebral. Trinity Sunday brought back chilling memories of confirmation classes, with words, words, difficult words imprisoned in the catechism, and then becoming imprisoned in the uncomprehending minds of teenage boys and girls. Trinity Sunday brought back chilling memories of the Athanasian Creed whose incomprehensible words had – to some extent – to be comprehended by theological students.

Over the years, as I became bolder and more experimental and, I hope, wiser, I came to see the Trinity not as something imprisoned in the catechism or in the Athanasian Creed, not as something that had to be taken out of some textbook once a year and dusted, but as something that was the very lifeblood of Christian discipleship, something to be experienced.

∾

One of the pitfalls of living in a place like this is that we are surrounded by natural beauty to such an extent that it is tempting to think of God only in terms of creation.

The sunrise this morning was as good as any I have seen: the sun coming up red behind the dark, almost black, cliffs across the Bay, and a pink reflection on the mill-pond water. An awareness of a marvellous slice of creation, and an awareness of God, somehow, behind the creation.

It is too easy in Lyme to stop there. In the midst of such an awareness can come another awareness: an awareness of the grace of Jesus of Nazareth, an awareness of the embrace of the Father, an awareness of the love and joy and peace being written upon the heart by the Holy Spirit. An awareness of the process of being recreated.

∾

A starting-point for me is receiving as a gift the spiritual energy emanating from the Holy Spirit. I am then enabled to profess Jesus as Lord, to say 'Jesus is Lord.' And I am enabled to cry 'Abba! Father!'

I particularly recollect a day on Church Beach when this

38

three-fold truth came to mean more to me than I can say. I pretty well fell down before Jesus of Nazareth and said, with St Thomas, 'My Lord and my God!', and I found myself saying over and over the words 'Abba! Father!'

In those few minutes I felt myself glimpsing the very foundation of Christian belief and practice and devotion. I felt myself as totally reconciled to God as I will ever be. I felt myself full of adoration and thanksgiving and confession and an awareness of other people's needs, and – simultaneously – full of a longing to become more fully what I already was. I was taken by surprise, as I always am when it comes to me afresh, by the knowedge of my status as a son of God. I glimpsed fleetingly the glorious liberty of the children of God. In those few minutes I felt that I could take on the world: nothing required of me would be too much, too great to achieve.

It only lasted for a few minutes and then it was gone. No, it wasn't gone. I carried it up the hill and down the path to the parish church, and it is with me always.

'Vicar, why do you believe in the Trinity?' In answering that question I might be too shy to refer to my own ephemeral experience of the Trinity on Church Beach, and I'd be more likely to refer to the early, halcyon days of the Franciscan movement when Francis and eleven friends were living in an abandoned hut near Assisi.

They had heard the call of Jesus of Nazareth – 'If any man would come after me, let him deny himself and take up his cross and follow me' – and were now following him more closely than anyone before or since. In their poverty and simplicity and humility, and bound together in love and joy and peace, they were living lives given – driven – by the Holy Spirit. They were surrounded by the beauty of the Umbrian countryside, and perhaps it was at this stage of his life that Francis began to venerate God as Father, as Father of all: Father of animals, Father of the rain-water that leaked into the hut, Father of the sun and moon, so that the wolf became Brother wolf, the water became Sister water, the sun became Brother sun, and the moon Sister moon.

I was standing at the water's edge, and the gentle remnants of the waves were almost lapping my shoes. The dawn was just breaking over the cliffs. As the sun rose and became progressively brighter it began to cast a reflection across the sea, and I began to feel the warmth of the sun, and all around me became illumined in daylight. It was a trinity of light. It was not one light but three. It was not three lights but one. I experienced the warmth of the sun, I was able to reach out and touch the reflection at the water's edge, and, after the pre-dawn darkness, I was able to see the cliffs and the sea and the beach and the bush around me.

There were a hundred children in the Parish Church at a Primary School assembly, with their teachers and some parents.

C. was in the organ loft playing the hymn 'Lord of the Dance' for us. For a while everything went as usual, and we sang 'Lord of the Dance'.

Then suddenly M. took the hands of two of the children, and they began skipping up the centre aisle and down one of the side aisles.

The idea was contagious, so very soon we had a whole lot of children not only singing, but also skipping up the centre aisle and down the side aisles, round and round the Parish Church.

It was one of my favourite moments in the Parish Church. I am not saying by any means that that would be my devotional style for ever and a day, but the moment was new and magical. There was something about it that revealed not only the innocence of childhood but the dynamism of the Christian faith.

We dance through the world together in the dance of Christian discipleship. The God of the world through which we dance is our Father, and we can feel ourselves bathed in his love. The invitation to dance comes from the Lord of the Dance, Jesus of Nazareth, and if we accept his invitation we dance to his tempo, fitting in with his steps, his ways, his ethics. What sets our feet tapping and induces us to dance is the Holy Spirit.

The eucharist is the sacrament of what is true everywhere and always.

We go up to the communion rail, and our breathing in of holy spirit enables us to receive into ourselves the love of the Father and the grace of Jesus of Nazareth.

And then the eucharist is over, and – hopefully – we bear fruit which may help to feed the world.

I sometimes sit quietly and think of myself as a branch that is part of the vine, as a Christian who is part of Christ.

I don't have to do anything for that to be true. It is true, and I simply receive the truth of it by faith with thanksgiving.

I sit there, a branch abiding in the vine, with the vine abiding in me; a Christian abiding in Christ, with Christ abiding in me.

Throughout the world there are other branches of the vine, other parts of Christ.

To all of us the sap brings the water and nutrients provided by the vinedresser, and the sugars given by the vine; to all of us the Holy Spirit brings the love of the Father and the grace of Christ. Thus are we enabled to bear fruit to feed the rest of creation.

What I have been trying to describe is the ecosystem which holds together the Trinity and Christians and the rest of creation. I feel myself to be part of a great dynamic whole.

Seeing myself in such a way helps me to relax; helps me to see that what I have to do is not all dependent on me but dependent on the dynamics of the vine. And seeing myself in such a way gives me confidence; gives me the confidence of knowing that what I am and what I stand for are very much greater than myself.

The eucharist is the sacrament of the ecosystem which binds together the Trinity and Christians and the rest of creation.

As the branches of the vine kneel at their various altar

rails, wherever the rails may be in the world, the Holy Spirit enables them – enables us – to receive into ourselves the love of the Father and the grace of Christ.

Then, leaving our altar rails, we go back to our Monday-to-Saturday responsibilities, and hopefully we bear fruit; and the fruit is borne – is meant to be borne – to feed mankind, to refresh mankind, to refresh the rest of creation.

Of course some branches of the vine are too dis-advantaged to have altar rails at which to kneel. They are, I am sure, the vine's most precious branches.

∽

On the Wednesday nights in Lent we say Compline in the Chapel. Compline is a quaint service that we dig out every Lent and put on in the Chapel for an ecumenical congre-gation.

Part of its quaintness lies in the number of times the service includes the Gloria:

'Glory be to the Father, and to the Son,
and to the Holy Spirit.'

Once I counted up the number of times the Gloria appears in the service, and I think the count came to six. Six times in a service lasting not much more than ten or fifteen minutes.

When one is not in the mood for it, it can seem exces-sive.

If, however, one is in the right devotional mood, then one can see that saying the Gloria a hundred times in a ten-minute service wouldn't be excessive: that all our life should, in one way or another, be devoted to giving glory to God – glory to the Father, and to the Son, and to the Holy Spirit.

∞

There are seven days in a week, and God has to be worshipped not just in the ceremonial worship in a church on a Sunday, but in one's work from Monday to Saturday.

There are 168 hours in a week, and God has to be worshipped not just in a church 'service' during one of the hours, but in one's service of God (and of course neighbour) during the other 167 hours.

If there is any separation between Sunday and the other six days, if there is any separation between the one hour and the other 167 hours, the mountains will witness a controversy that the Lord has with his people. If there is such a controversy it is one of the most serious and fundamental controversies in Christian discipleship.

∞

One of my favourite collects is that for a Harvest Festival. After giving thanks, we go on to ask that we may use the harvest rightly, to God's glory, for our own well-being, and for the relief of those in need.

What does it mean to use the harvest to God's glory? Is there some religious circle into which we retire for the purpose of giving glory to God? I don't think so. To use the harvest to God's glory involves using it for our own well-being and using it for the relief of those in need. Then, if we are doing that, we shall be using it to God's glory.

It is easy to have high-flown ideas about God's glory, but God's glory has to be earthed. If we exist on a diet of salted crisps and Belgian chocolates we shall not be using the harvest to God's glory, and if we hog the world's harvest for ourselves we shall not be using it to God's glory. The only way – the only way I know of – of using the harvest to God's glory is by using it for our own well-being and for the relief of those in need.

There is no point in directing fine, high-flown words in public worship to God's glory unless we are filling the phrase with meaning in our lives, unless our lives are being devoted to the furtherance of God's glory. There is no point in saying piously in the Sunday liturgy 'Glory be to God on high' unless we are doing everything we can from Monday to Saturday to live lives to God's glory. The way to give glory to God is by the way we live.

∾

To my mind the most inspiring picture of worship is the worship of one of the wise men in Rembrandt's painting 'The Adoration of the Magi'. He has fallen to his knees and is worshipping the child lying in Mary's arms. The painting is full of light and shade, with most of the light, wonderful gold light, bathing the three figures of wise man and mother and child. The old man has forgotten about his arthritic hips and osteoporotic spine, and he is on his knees in a posture of total reverence and adoration. He is totally concentrated on the child, with his hands held together in front of him in an attitude of prayer. It is a picture of sublime, ineffable worship.

Such worship does not have to take place in an ornate

church, or in a church at all, and it does not have to be expressed in showy language. In fact it is most at home in a stable or upper room or on a hillside or beach or in any poor place.

∾

My needs as far as worship is concerned are modest. All I want is to be able to *remember* Jesus of Nazareth in the eucharist with something of the devotion of Rembrandt's wise man. I need no grand setting: just a setting that is as consistent as possible with the settings to which Jesus was accustomed. I need hardly any words: no lip worship, just worship from the heart, affirming the inwardness of true worship.

∾

This Christmas my nice worship is being rather spoilt by having a poster pinned to the notice board in the porch of the Parish Church. It is a photograph – a large one – of two teenagers sleeping rough in a subway, and beside the photograph are the words 'It's our birthday – but we're not celebrating.'

The poster is a few feet away from our beautiful Christmas crib, showing the child and Mary and Joseph in the stable, with straw all around them, and the shepherds and their sheep and the three wise men.

There is a distance of a few feet between the two teenagers in the subway and the child in his crib.

All through the Christmas season the poster will be on the notice board pleading the cause of the poor and needy. It is disturbing.

Is there a link between the homeless teenagers and the child we are worshipping?

Yes, they should be totally linked. No separation should exist between them. We should be investing the teenagers and the child with reverent worth. There should be no separation between our response to the teenagers and our response to the child. The love we are giving to the child should go hand in hand with love given to the teenagers. The homage we pay to the child must not be so 'religious' that it excludes the teenagers.

❧

There is a man who used to visit disabled people each Saturday, doing handyman jobs for them, mowing their lawns, that sort of thing. His wife had died, he had no children, and he liked helping people. He didn't expect or accept any payment for what he did.

He thought it would be great if he could take his disabled friends for drives, therefore he bought a car, a second-hand car, a fairly old one.

To begin with, it was great. He put three people in the car each Saturday morning and took them to the beach for an ice cream, then in the afternoon he took three others into the country.

One Saturday he thought his car looked rather grubby, so he spent the day vacuum cleaning it and washing and polishing it, and by the end of the day it looked like new.

Except that the washing and polishing had shown up some rust and he thought he should deal with it. During the week he bought some rust-removing materials and a touch-up stick, and he spent the next Saturday de-rusting the car.

The following Saturday he went to the disabled folk and showed them his car, and they all thought he had done a splendid job on it and he felt very proud of it.

During the week he heard that there would be a rally that Saturday in the next county, and he went to it to see whether he could pick up any tips for keeping his car in good order.

He picked up so many tips that he spent the whole of the next Saturday, and the next, and the next in doing minor repair jobs on the car, and jazzing it up with various gadgets he had bought at the rally.

And then he decided that it was looking so good that he should build a garage for it.

He saw his disabled friends at Christmas-time, and it was good to see them. But that was the last time he saw them because he spent months building the garage in his spare time. He missed them of course, and he still sent them birthday cards, but now he seemed to be so busy. But you should just see his car. It really looks very good, and it really goes very well.

❧

We may not see the need for change in ourselves, but others may see that need.

Disadvantaged people in this country – the unemployed and others like them. Do they not sometimes look at us and see a lot of room in us for change, room for turning from our apparent indifference to their welfare, room for turning towards them with greater concern?

Disadvantaged people in other parts of the world – the sick and hungry and refugees. Do they not perhaps glimpse the kind of lives we are living and see some room for change, room for turning from our relative indifference and superfluity and privilege, room for turning towards them more fully?

People outside the churches. Do they not look at us, insider churchmen, and see some room for change, room for turning from all the power and triviality and materialism by which we have been seduced, room for turning towards the way walked by the crucified?

∾

As I grow older I find that I believe more and more firmly in less and less. Whereas in my youth I would perhaps have gone over the top to fight for line 16 or line 34 of one of the creeds, now in my old age I'd be content to settle for the creed of the early church: the confession of Jesus as Lord. That is what I would now die for – Jesus as Lord.

∾

Today has been a bad day. After the collect for the day ('. . . grant that as your holy angels always serve you in heaven, so by your appointment they may help and defend us on earth'), there was a sermon about angels which made no attempt whatsoever to help me or the rest of the congregation to understand where the mention of angels fits in to Christian belief. The people of the Bible, the preacher said, believed in angels, so why shouldn't we? But goodness gracious, the people of the Bible also believed in a three-storey universe, and the preacher surely wasn't saying that we should also. Or was he? It is

49

incredible that a preacher can at the end of the twentieth-century preach a sermon in which a *literal* belief in angels is assumed.

So, Dell, back to the chapter on angels in John Robinson's *But That I Can't Believe!* '. . . they are ways of representing or picturing certain convictions – theological convictions, not scientific convictions – about the meaning of life'. The book was published thirty years ago, but we ministers don't yet seem to have absorbed a fraction of it.

∽

He came down from heaven.

He was worshipped by angels.

Then all will be united and perfected in heaven, save what has been lost to hell.

. . . when he comes again in glory and judgment.

. . . the angel Gabriel told the Virgin Mary . . .

Extracts from a seventeenth-century book? From an early twentieth-century book? No, they are from a widely-used book of services and prayers published seven years ago.

We must work harder to create an indigenous liturgy: indigenous to the world in which we live, indigenous to the world of Copernicus and Galileo and Darwin and Leakey. And if such a liturgy cannot be created, then we must introduce new Christians to traditional liturgical words with more explanation and honesty, so that they do not fall into the trap of taking the language literally.

∽

It was St Thomas's Day, in a year in which St Thomas's Day fell on a Sunday. We had been celebrating Thomas, his honesty, his integrity, and then finally his cry of belief: 'My Lord and my God!' Then . . .

Then immediately we went on to the creed, and soon afterwards to the hymn 'Firmly I believe and truly'. At that point we seemed to turn our backs on Thomas, on his honest doubt, on his struggling and burgeoning belief. We seemed to be requiring people to believe too much, we seemed to be requiring people to take too much on board all at once. People's minds become cluttered up with umpteen bits of belief. We overload them.

Anyone reading my words may think that I want to ditch the mystery. Of course I don't. I want the mystery to be exposed, to be stripped of the frippery in which it is clothed, so that a new generation of thinking Christians can begin to see the beauty of the mystery in something of its nakedness and not be obstructed by the frippery.

For example I don't want to ditch St Francis of Assisi. Far from it. When I commend St Francis to a congregation I want people to be able to distinguish between the time-less spirituality of the man and the thirteenth-century beliefs in which the spirituality was clothed. St Francis was a man of his time. Throughout the stories about his life there are assumptions about the kind of world in which he lived: a three-storey world of visions and miracles and angels and demons. I don't want to ditch St Francis. What I want is for people to be able to see his timeless beauty and not be obstructed by the thirteenth-century clothes clinging to him.

And most of all I want people to be able to see the beauty of Jesus of Nazareth and not be put off by the first-century and fourth-century world in which he is presented.

∾

I believe that the tree of defeat became the tree of glory, as the liturgy says. But doctrine and liturgy have tended to make of the defeat and glory two entirely separate events, and that is one of the ways in which we have become unstuck. The tree of defeat is the tree of glory only in so far as it is filled with a fresh depth of meaning, only in so far as it is seen with the eye of faith.

∾

I try to read the Gospels as first-century documents, and I try to say the Apostles' and Nicene Creeds as fourth-century documents. In reading them and saying them I try to extract their kernel from their surrounding shell.

The shell consists, for example, of assumptions about cosmology, assumptions about the cause of disease, assumptions about miraculous happenings.

The shell is cracked with nutcrackers, but the kernel is kept and eaten.

∾

Belief is more than cerebral belief, belief with the mind, belief that such-and-such is so.

One can profess Jesus of Nazareth to be the way, the truth, and the life. But it is so easy to say that. Words can come so easily. More than words is required if belief is to be belief. The way has to be walked, the truth has to be dwelt in, the life has to be lived. But even more than that. The way, the truth, and the life are a person, and belief is not just cerebral belief about him but commitment to him.

St Thomas might have said coolly to Jesus 'My Lord and my God!', indicating his cerebral belief about him. But I think more than that was involved. I think Thomas probably fell down before Jesus and exclaimed 'My Lord and my God!' in a very different sort of way, putting the whole of himself into the words, committing himself to him, entrusting himself to him.

Euagelio (that we cal gospel) is a greke worde, and signyfyth good, mery, glad and joyfull tydings, that maketh a mannes hert glad, and maketh hym synge, daunce and leepe for joye.

William Tyndale

The God of Christianity is so often perceived not as good, mery, glad and joyfull tydings but as bad tidings. God is condemnatory, punishing, malignant. Such a view is held by countless people, and it has a damaging effect on their psyches, their inner selves, their mental health.

God is perceived as 'taking' people ('Forasmuch as it hath pleased Almighty God of his great mercy to take unto himself the soul of our dear brother here departed . . .') and punishing people ('God is punishing me . . . He's punishing me for having led such a selfish life', says a man injured in an accident) and inflicting cancer on people ('I hate him', says a widow, 'after what he did to John').

An article in *The Times* was a final straw for me. It came after the tragedy of Dunblane and I'm sure was meant to be a helpful article. But in the article a bishop implied that Dunblane was something God allowed to happen. To my way of thinking, allowing something to happen is the next best thing to causing it to happen. The idea that God allowed Dunblane to happen is at best a tired, worn-out idea, at worst an obscenity. Something snapped in me when I read that article. I realized I didn't believe in the bishop's God.

Rembrandt's painting 'The Ascension' has Jesus ascending through space on a little cloud, with angels pushing the cloud upwards, and people watching from down below.

That literalism is perhaps excusable in the work of a man living in the seventeenth-century. But I have seen a similar literalism in a late twentieth-century film, and that is inexcusable because now we should know better.

From such a literalism I'd want to run a mile.

We must make it plain that a literal belief in the travelling done by Jesus between heaven and earth (coming down from heaven, ascending into heaven, and coming again) has no place in our Christian discipleship.

There's always a first time for everything, and I think that one day a minister will be sued for the first time for misleading someone, for deceiving him, for teaching him in such a way that he was encouraged to accept as his cosmology the alternative cosmology of the Bible. Such teaching, on the surface, may not seem damaging. But it is. In the course of time it may precipitate a crisis in the individual. He may cease to believe in the three-storey universe in which his faith has been wrapped, and his faith is so closely wrapped in the alternative cosmology that in shedding the cosmology he sheds his faith. Great harm has been done to him, and he sues his minister.

∽

'Jesus Christ who came down into this world . . .'

'Jesus came to earth.'

'Jesus was sent into the world to . . .'

Those words were all written or said by colleagues in the past few months, at the end of the twentieth century, as if they believed in a three-storey universe.

If we don't believe in that, then we must say so, in order to avoid deceiving people. We must come out of the closet.

Jesus didn't come down into this world, he didn't come to earth, he was not sent into the world. He was *born*. Let's rather talk about him being born, and see where that leads us.

∽

*The former Bishop of Durham, Dr David Jenkins,
was amazed and shattered by reactions to the
questions he raised about the virgin birth and the
resurrection at the beginning of his episcopacy . . .
'I was . . . furious with the fact that, for instance,
fellow bishops, many of whom I know hold the
same views as me, didn't put their heads over the
parapet.'*

It is surprising to me that Bishop Jenkins could have been
so savagely treated for expressing his opinion that Mary
was a *young woman* who conceived and bore a son, and
that the resurrection of Jesus was not a literal physio-
logical event of flesh and blood and bones which left the
tomb empty. And it is surprising to me that his fellow
bishops, or some of them, didn't put their heads over the
parapet.

The subject can be tackled in a very gentle way. I myself
have always said to a congregation that they are free to
believe in *this* way, or in *that* way, or they can sit
honourably on the fence and say 'I don't know'. Speaking
in such a way to people can provide a gentle way for them
to begin thinking about matters such as the virgin birth
and resurrection. The boat doesn't have to be rocked. On
the other hand, the boat is going to have to be rocked at
some time or another.

∾

Why is it that Modernists for the last forty years have had to endure such bitter attacks? As I seek an answer I am reminded of an incident of my schooldays. Outside one of the great markets in Birmingham sat an old dame selling oranges at four a penny. She held four oranges piled up in her hand. 'Turn them over, mother,' said a realist schoolboy friend as we passed her, to receive in turn a volley of abuse. She resented the insinuation that her stock was mouldy, the more fiercely because the insinuation was true. The Christian traditionalist, whether Catholic or Fundamentalist, was not so clearly aware of the causes of his wrath. When the Modernist expounded what he knew to be true, the traditionalist thought him an infidel, who rejected venerable beliefs. Yet the fierceness of his invective arose from a secret misgiving – a feeling rather than a thought that his own beliefs were, like those oranges, unsound.

E. W. Barnes

A handout advertising a cycle of mediaeval mystery plays describes them as containing 'the whole sweep of History from the Creation to the Last Judgment as seen by Mediaeval man, and man's place within that history . . .'

Mediaeval man might have seen, for example, the creation stories at the beginning of the Bible as historical accounts, but surely we don't; and if we don't, we should say so more clearly. Adam and Eve are not historical figures. They are generic terms meaning man and woman, John and Mary, you and me, everyman and everywoman everywhere and always.

Only seventy years ago a schoolteacher in America was taken to court and tried for teaching Darwin's theory of evolution. The story is told in two film versions of the play *Inherit the Wind*. In both versions, I think, the story ends with the schoolmaster's lawyer left alone in the courtroom. He begins to pack up his belongings. He picks up a copy of Darwin's *The Origin of Species* in one hand, and a copy of the Bible in the other. He looks at them, he ponders over them, he kind of mentally weighs them in his hands. Then he slaps them together and carries them out of the courtroom.

Holding both *The Origin of Species* and the Bible is surely symbolic of the way in which we approach our Christian discipleship – with that sort of coherence, with that sort of integrity, with that sort of congruence. *The Origin of Species* (or any other scientific textbook or encyclopaedia) and the Bible are giving us different kinds of information, different kinds of meaning, and we've got to hold them both together.

It has been quite difficult being a priest who is aware of living in a transitional period and who has felt himself very much in the middle.

On the one hand I have felt locked into a conventional belief by the language of the Bible, creeds, liturgy, collects and hymns, and the key which turns the lock to provide an escape hasn't always been readily available; and if it has been available, I haven't always wanted to use it for fear of rocking the boat, for fear of hurting people, for fear of destroying their lifelong faith, for fear of deserting my role as pastor.

On the other hand, there has always been the longing to climb further on the slopes of the huge hill of truth, and to try to express more forcefully what is to be found there.

In a different way it was rather like that in Namibia in pre-Independence days. Caught in the middle in a different sort of way. On the one hand the apartheid regime wasn't right, and on the other hand the armed liberation struggle didn't seem right. Therefore there was the feeling of being caught in the middle, powerless, hammered from both sides, continuing to do what one could do to hold people together, to create to the best of one's ability a non-racial congregation, but all the time feeling oneself to be a powerless pastor.

Caught in the middle, there has been a good deal of pain, a good deal of agony.

Some things are very difficult to understand, and it is helpful if the minister can share with his congregation the difficulty he has in understanding them. Furthermore the minister should warn people not to accept from anyone any explanations that are simple and glib. There should always be an honoured place in ministry for 'I don't know, I don't know what this means, I don't know what that means. I can look up to see what the scholars say about this or that, but then you may have the difficult task of choosing between different opinions.'

An honest approach is far better than the across-the-board pretence of certainty that so often prevails. An appearance of perpetual certainty seems to go hand in hand with a kind of mindlessness which should never, never be part of Christian discipleship. How can anyone at the end of the twentieth century not be agnostic about various things?

I should be quite happy to be called a Christian humanist, providing the word 'humanist' is used in the sense in which the Renaissance thinkers were called humanists.

If my understanding is correct, the Renaissance humanists were not like our present-day humanists. If we use the word 'humanist' today we generally mean by it someone who is opposed to religion. But that is not what the Renaissance humanists were. They didn't reject Christianity. What they did was to welcome the fresh air blowing away the superstition and authoritarianism of previous centuries; to welcome the fresh air blowing into the Bible and enabling scholars to get a clearer view of what it was about; to welcome the fresh air blowing into the study of man and the universe.

I'd be quite happy to be called a Christian atheist, providing the word 'atheist' is used in the sense in which it was used to describe the early Christians. They refused to worship the old gods, they refused to worship the gods of the Roman state. And so they were regarded as atheists.

There was a time when I found myself rejecting innumerable gods, for example the god up there, the taskmaster god, the malignant god.

In rejecting the old gods I felt released. Oh, what a relief it was!

Then, more soberly, I began to wonder whether it did not perhaps mean the end of the line for me as a priest. After all, I was paid my monthly stipend because I believed, and what did I now believe? Having thrown out the gods one by one, did I believe any longer in any god? 'Lord,' I found myself paradoxically praying, 'Lord, I must be an atheist.'

It was a bad moment. Fortunately, however, I was soon rescued by the thought that the early Christians had been called atheists because of their rejection of the old Roman gods.

I didn't have much time to reflect on my newfound atheism because of what happened early the next day.

I went down to Church Beach below the Parish Church, from where one can look across Lyme Bay to where the sun rises over Golden Cap. It was a bitterly cold morning, and I had my hands in my pockets.

And I found . . . I found that I had to take my hands out of my pockets.

For anyone of my generation, having one's hands in one's pockets in the presence of another is disrespectful. And I found myself to be in the presence of another.

My awareness of God was so powerful that I couldn't possibly have remained standing there with my hands in my pockets.

'That's most peculiar,' I thought to myself. 'That's quite

amazing. I'm supposed to be an atheist, but perhaps it was just the old gods that I rejected and not God.'

There I was, standing on a beach in the bitter wind, unable to put my hands in my pockets.

And ever since that day I have never, on Church Beach, been able to put my hands in my pockets.

∽

The morning on which I thought I was an atheist was a morning on which I felt birth-pangs. I had thought it was going to be the end, the end of me as a priest, but it turned out to be a beginning.

What was delivered that day? What came out of the bloody mess?

In brief, a fresh belief in a Trinitarian God, and an exalted view of humankind, or rather the possibilities within humankind.

I found myself falling down, metaphorically speaking, and saying 'My Lord and my God!' I recalled St Paul's words: 'No one can say "Jesus is Lord" except by the Holy Spirit', therefore it occurred to me that the Holy Spirit was revering Jesus of Nazareth through me.

I found myself crying 'Abba! Father!' I recalled St Paul's words about the Holy Spirit in our hearts crying 'Abba! Father!', therefore it occurred to me that the Holy Spirit was revering the Father through me.

I found myself loving other people rather more than before. I didn't feel that I had the capacity within me to produce that love, and I thought that it might be the Holy Spirit, the one whose fruit is love and joy and peace, loving through me – and the hungry, thirsty, sick person being loved was perhaps none other than Jesus himself. Was it the Holy Spirit loving Jesus through me?

If there was anything in these ideas, then I had an exalted status. Not only was I a son of God but I was necessary to God. I was fulfilling an exalted purpose. The very relations within the dynamics of the Trinity were dependent on me. I was a meeting-place for the persons of the Trinity, a channel for their interaction. I was facilitating the love that existed among the persons of the Trinity.

All that may sound fantastic, but that is what emerged on the day when I thought I was an atheist. That is what I was left with.

❧

I cannot say much about the God I was left with. More or less all I can describe is the effect felt.

A blind man may struggle to describe the sun, but finds it easier to describe the effect of the sun. He describes the warmth it gives, the sunburn it can cause, the outdoor living it enables, the summer barbecues and swimming.

He may be content to leave the description of the sun to the textbooks and encyclopaedias. What he himself knows and treasures is what the sun gives him.

❧

Not only do I find it difficult to define or describe God, but any attempted definition or description has its dangers. God defined is reduced to the limits of one's mind; God described is reduced to the limits of one's words.

At the beginning of the musical *The Sound of Music* the nuns in the abbey try to communicate the truth about the high-spirited nun Maria, and they cannot. They sing:

How do you catch a cloud and pin it down? . . .
How do you keep a wave upon the sand? . . .
How do you hold a moonbeam in your hand?

∾

All one can do is to describe hearing a still small voice, and wrapping one's face in one's mantle. All one can do is to describe seeing a burning bush, and putting off one's shoes from one's feet. All one can do is to describe seeing a man on a cross, or a man cooking fish and bread on a beach at daybreak.

∾

Despite what I have written I am not one for much God-talk. In fact I should be quite happy to write the word God as G-d, perhaps because I cannot give full meaning to the whole word God, perhaps because I regard the word as so sacred that it should not be written, perhaps because of my reverence for what lies behind the word.

∾

When one does try to define G-d one finds that the object of one's definition has slipped through the definition, like an ox slipping through a lasso one has thrown to catch him, and running away.

One is left with a non-definition like that of St Augustine of Hippo:

God is an infinite circle whose centre is everywhere and whose circumference is nowhere.

The consequences of such a definition or non-definition are limitless.

∾

If one believes that God is an infinite circle whose centre is everywhere and whose circumference is nowhere – if one believes that, what then is religion all about?

If one is told that religion is about what happens within a particular circle, within a particular building or structure or organization or church or institution, what becomes of religion if there is no 'within', if the 'within' has been blown to the four corners of the cosmos? Religion cannot be confined within any 'within', within any limits, within any circle – because there is no circle. The circle doesn't exist because its centre is everywhere and its circumference is nowhere. Both centre and circumference have been blown away by the desert wind of the Spirit of God.

Religion must then be about the whole of life. Religion, stretching to take in the whole of life, ceases to exist as a circumscribed entity in itself.

After hearing me muse on this matter someone may say to me 'Then in your view there is nothing sacred any more; you are not retaining anything sacred.' Oh no, my friend, you've got it wrong. In my view *everything* becomes sacred.

∾

Thou art a sea without a shore,
A sun without a sphere;
Thy time is now and evermore,
Thy place is everywhere.

John Mason

I would certainly want to exclude from my belief system any superstition or crude supernaturalism.

I certainly wouldn't go to a fairground to have my palm read, nor would I look up my horoscope in a magazine, nor listen to Mystic Meg's predictions. I certainly wouldn't throw bones or examine the entrails of a sacrificial animal or ask questions of a ouija-board. There is no room in my belief system for a three-storey universe or angels or demons. Mary was a young woman, not a virgin, and the empty tomb was not a literal event. No room for reincarnation. I'd be happy to accept the view of a reputable scientist about the physical creation of the universe. At heart I am not only a priest but an unholy, sceptical doctor, and nothing that is benevolently scientific frightens me.

The natural, the ordinary is sufficiently wonderful and can be suffused with the spiritual. My rejection of superstition and crude supernaturalism does not, I believe, exclude from my life a spiritual fountainhead, a penumbra of mystery.

In the course of following Jesus of Nazareth we discover the depth of his humanity, the depth of his feeling, the depth of his wisdom, the depth of his suffering. That is how we can speak of his divinity: because we have come to perceive the depth of his humanity.

One of the reasons for my rage against religion is that the natural, the ordinary is undervalued. Another world – the supernatural world – is superimposed on the existing natural world.

For example, ordinary ground is not good enough to bury people in. It has to be consecrated. And that is a slur put upon the ordinary, the natural. I rage against that. In my view consecrated ground is not just the ground pointed out by the notices one sees in churchyards and cemeteries – 'This is consecrated ground: please treat it as such.' No, all ground all over the planet must be treated as such: our backyards, Broad Street, the countryside, the rain forests.

What is needed is not the superimposition of the super-natural on the natural but a deepening of the natural, a deepening perception of the natural.

If there is a supernatural and if it is something different from the natural, then it is different in depth. It is not different in the way that blue is different from red. It is different in the way that navy blue is different from pale blue.

But to close the door upon any possibility of a supernatural force breaking through to the natural would not be my style. For one thing it would seem to diminish the lives of people such as St Francis of Assisi.

One must always leave open the possibility that

'There are more things in heaven and earth, Horatio,
Than are dreamt of in your philosophy.'

I hope that for me G-d will remain G-d, mysterious, ineffable, unfathomable.

❧

I've got a card, with a black and white picture on it. Black and white blobs really. Nothing more than that. Black and white blobs.

Each time I come across it in a drawer I pick it up and stare at it intently, knowing that it contains more meaning than just black and white blobs. Then suddenly I see that it is a picture of the head and shoulders of a man.

Each time I have forgotten what the head and shoulders are going to look like, and where they are going to appear in the picture. Each time it is a surprise when they suddenly come into focus.

The card contains the following inscription on the back:

The story that is told about this picture is of a Chinese photographer, deeply troubled religiously, who took a picture of the melting snow with black earth showing through. When he developed it, he

68

*was amazed to see in it the face of Christ, full of
tenderness and love, and he became a Christian.*

*It may take you a long time to see the face, but that
difficulty is, perhaps, a symbol of the effort that
must be made to find him in our world. Once
found, however, as in the picture, he dominates the
scene, and one wonders how it was possible to
miss him.*

I think perception of the supernatural can be a little like
that. As one concentrates on the natural, it suddenly
appears to rearrange itself to reveal new, deeper meaning.

*To see a World in a Grain of Sand
And a Heaven in a Wild Flower,
Hold Infinity in the palm of your hand
And Eternity in an hour.*

William Blake

What is it that happens on Christmas Eve?

By nature he is a rather loutish fellow, thinking
generally of no one but himself. On the days before
Christmas he is particularly churlish because his business
involves a good deal of Christmas trade, and the crowds
and long hours make him disagreeable.

Then when he shuts the shop at lunchtime on Christmas
Eve he becomes a different man, going out in the car to

buy a Christmas tree, and gifts for the family, and flowers for his mother and father.

What happens surprises his family and surprises himself.

He himself would say that he hasn't got the capacity within himself to generate the sort of love he feels and shows each Christmas Eve. He shrugs it off and says that it is the spirit of Christmas that can sweep even a selfish, loutish fellow like himself off his feet and make him do what he never thinks he has it in him to do.

Does it happen on Christmas Eve as a result of something which originates within the person, or as a result of something which comes from beyond him?

O world invisible, we view thee,
　O world intangible, we touch thee,
O world unknowable, we know thee,
　Inapprehensible, we clutch thee!

Does the fish soar to find the ocean,
　The eagle plunge to find the air—
That we ask of the stars in motion
　If they have rumour of thee there?

Not where the wheeling systems darken,
　And our benumbed conceiving soars!—
The drift of pinions, would we hearken,
　Beats at our own clay-shuttered doors.

The angels keep their ancient places;—
　Turn but a stone, and start a wing!
'Tis ye, 'tis your estrangèd faces,
　That miss the many-splendoured thing.

But (when so sad thou canst not sadder)
  Cry;—and upon thy so sore loss
Shall shine the traffic of Jacob's ladder
  Pitched betwixt Heaven and Charing Cross.

Yea, in the night, my Soul, my daughter,
  Cry,—clinging Heaven by the hems;
And lo, Christ walking on the water
  Not of Gennesareth, but Thames!

Francis Thompson

ᔕ

Let us hope that one day Christianity will again make sense to thinking people. Meanwhile, that day must be prepared for.

The day must be prepared for in the sort of way in which the Battle of Britain was prepared for in the pre-war years by men such as Hugh Dowding who from 1936 was commander-in-chief, Fighter Command. This involved, among other things, erecting a chain of radar stations along the English coast and linking them to a central command station.

This is the sort of preparation that must be going on now – that is, I suppose, going on now – in order to prepare for the day when Christianity can be presented as a credible belief to twentieth-century – soon twenty-first-century – people. A twenty-first-century God will have to be presented, not a first-century or fourth-century or thirteenth-century God. Much groundwork is now needed.

ᔕ

When all is said and done, the imperative is not to believe or disbelieve that the birth was literally virgin or that the resurrection was literally bodily, not to believe or disbelieve in the supernatural. The imperative is 'Follow me . . .', to live a life following him.

∞

If it were proved that there was no such thing as the supernatural I don't think I'd be fazed by the proof. I would, I believe, be able to take what I know to be true about my life and move on and fit into a revised view of G-d. I'd continue to walk on the slopes of the huge hill where truth stands. I'd continue to stand on that rock of love on which the whole universe is constructed. I'd continue to go in heart and mind even unto Galilee and Judaea. I'd continue to *remember* Jesus of Nazareth. I'd continue to be willing to die for my profession of Jesus as Lord.

∞

I expect the next assault upon so-called orthodox Christian belief to be upon life after life. Thus far it has mainly been the turn of the virgin birth and empty tomb. Soon it will be the turn of so-called everlasting life.

The assault will at first be upon the facile ways in which the idea of heaven and life after life has been presented. The following are just a few of the ways in my very recent experience.

A friend, on being told by me of the death of another friend: 'Hurray, another little new angel in heaven.'

Said after the death of a friend with a fine singing voice: 'She is now singing in heaven with the angels and archangels.'

A child's words, quoted – very much with approval – by a minister in an address at Granny's funeral: 'Granny will be seeing Grandpa again and my budgie and guinea pig.'

A departed lady's words, spoken in heaven and now quoted by a minister in his address at her funeral: 'She's saying to us "Cheer up; through Christ you can come here too".'

Said by a member of the congregation after a funeral: 'He's OK. He's up there looking down on us.'

A bishop preaching at a young people's service: 'The bodily presence of Jesus was withdrawn into heaven.'

A minister in a funeral address: 'It will be good to see our loved ones and to see Jesus face to face.'

The beautiful words from John 3.16 sung by the chorus in Stainer's 'The Crucifixion' are wrong:

God so loved the world, that he gave his only begotten Son, that whosoever believeth in him should not perish, but have everlasting life.

Not everlasting life but *eternal* life:

> *God so loved the world that he gave his only Son,*
> *that whoever believes in him should not perish but*
> *have eternal life.*

Eternal life is a quality of life rather than a duration of life, and it can be apprehended here and now, it can be lived here and now.

For the most part Christians have a big stake in the idea of everlasting life. I think there will have to be a massive shift in emphasis from the idea of everlasting life to the idea of eternal life. I fear that when that happens a great number of people will be hurt.

∾

> *Almighty God, who through your only-begotten*
> *Son Jesus Christ overcame death and opened to us*
> *the gate of everlasting life . . .*

I do not believe that he opened to us the gate of everlasting life. He opened to us the gate of eternal life, which is something very different.

∾

The final verse of 'The Canticle of the Sun' by St Francis:

> *All praise be yours, my Lord, for Sister Death,*
>   *from whose embrace no mortal can escape.*
> *Woe to those who die in mortal sin!*
> *Happy those she finds doing your most holy will!*
> *The second death can do no harm to them.*

Many years before and in the intervening years Francis had died the first death when he had responded to the words of Jesus of Nazareth as reported in Matt. 16. 24f.: 'If any man would come after me, let him deny himself and take up his cross and follow me. For whoever would save his life will lose it, and whoever loses his life for my sake will find it.' That had been his entry into eternal life. That had been the really significant death.

Now the second death facing him could hold no terrors for him, could do him no harm.

In a sermon preached in Cambridge six weeks before he died from cancer, Bishop John Robinson said this, *inter alia*:

> *'Preparing for death' is not the other-worldly pious exercise stamped upon our minds by Victorian sentimentality, turning away from the things of earth for the things of 'heaven'. Rather, for the Christian it is preparing for 'eternal life', which means real living, more abundant life, which is begun, continued, though not ended, now. And this means it is about quality of life not quantity . . .*

In the castle of my soul there is a little postern gate
Where, when I enter, I am in the presence of God.
In a moment, in a turning of a thought,
I am where God is.
When I meet God there, all life gains a new
*   meaning,*
Small things become great, and great things small.
Lowly and despised things are shot through with
*   glory.*
My troubles seem but pebbles on the road,
My joys seem like the everlasting hills,
All my fever is gone in the great peace of God,
And I pass through the door from Time into
*   Eternity.*

Walter Rauschenbusch

So it is not so much a question of the eternal following the temporal as the eternal breaking through into the temporal.

The collect gets it wrong, I think, when it encourages one to pray that

> *we may so pass through things temporal that we finally lose not the things eternal.*

Those words could encourage one to believe that the eternal is reached only at the end of a long hard slog of temporal existence. A temporal drudge of threescore years and ten, and then the eternal.

No, the eternal breaks through into the threescore years and ten, like wave after wave breaking on to a beach.

Jesus said, 'Father . . . this is eternal life: to know you the only true God, and Jesus Christ whom you have sent.'

That is what eternal life is: knowing God. And knowing God is knowing God, something rather different from simply knowing about God, something rather more intimate. It is knowledge written upon one's heart.

To have given me self-consciousness but for an hour in a world so breathless with beauty would have been enough. But thou hast preserved it within me for twenty years now and more, and hast crowned it with the joy of this summer of summers. And so come what may, whether life or death, and, if death, whether bliss unimaginable or nothingness, I thank thee and bless thy name. Author unknown

'Why do you believe in him?'
'He set me free', he said simply.
'From what?'
'From myself', he said, as though it was the most natural thing in the world for a crooked tax-man with a caricature of a face to discuss metaphysics in front of a television camera.
'How did he do that?'
'He forgave me. Met me in the street and accepted me, and forgave me for being the sort of man I am.'

Zacchaeus, interviewed in *The Davidson Affair*

There's a freedom about being a branch of the vine. A branch is a branch. That is what it is. It doesn't have to strive to be a branch, and in that lack of striving there is a freedom that many of us need to cultivate. All the branch has to do is to recognize that it is a branch. There's a givenness about it. It can just relax in the branchness of being a branch, and fit in with being a branch, and let the sap bring to its cells the water and essential nutrients provided by the vinedresser and the sugars manufactured in the leaves. Just relax, branch, and trust that your cells are being fed by the rich sap, and you will bear grapes.

A sense of freedom is built in to my being a son of God. There is a freedom from striving, but more than that: I can have a foretaste of the glorious liberty which is a positive, intrinsic part of the lives of children of God.

I cannot become a son by striving to become a son. There is a givenness about it. I discover that I am a son. During the discovery the Holy Spirit is helping me to acknowledge Jesus as Lord, and helping me to cry 'Abba! Father!', and the sense of freedom is very much an integral part of this experience of being a son caught up in the dynamics of the Trinity. Where the Spirit of the Lord is, there is freedom.

A woman came in, who had a bad name in the town . . . She had brought with her an alabaster jar of ointment . . . Her tears fell on Jesus' feet, and she wiped them away with her hair; then she covered his feet with kisses and anointed them with the ointment . . . Jesus said 'Her sins, her many sins, must have been forgiven her, or she would not have shown such great love.'

(Luke 7.36ff.)

I am one of those who believe that the woman poured out her devotion as a result of having been forgiven by Jesus some time before. She had encountered Jesus, and he had released her from her bad name, he had set her free – and *that* was the power, the impetus, the momentum that enabled her now to go to Jesus and pour out her devotion. She had been forgiven much, therefore she became able to love much.

The first half of the story – which is not included in the gospel story about the woman – is about what Jesus did for her, what he gave her. And the second half of the story is her response to what happened in the first half: her grace-fired response.

The two halves of discipleship must be in place and joined together.

The first half can be seen in what was done for Zacchaeus, what was given to Zacchaeus – and his acceptance of what was done for him and given to him.

The second half can be glimpsed when Zacchaeus said to Jesus, 'Behold, Lord, the half of my goods I give to the

79

poor; and if I have defrauded anyone of anything, I restore it fourfold.'

Some people skip the first half, and they go straight into the second half, the good works half – and their good works are then dry and barren and a great drag.

Other people get stuck in the first half, and they become turned in on a self-indulgent wallowing in the beautiful thing that has happened to them. They forget that that is only a first half which is meant to lead on to a second half. Therefore they don't take off their Sunday suits and roll up their sleeves and tackle the task of creating a better world.

It is only when the two halves of discipleship come together that one can say 'Today salvation has come to this house, to this man, to this woman.'

Jesus said to him, 'You shall love the Lord your God with all your heart, and with all your soul, and with all your mind. This is the great and first commandment. And a second is like it, You shall love your neighbour as yourself.' (Matt. 22.37f.)

In those words Jesus sums up what is required of us. He sets before us our task. It is the task for which we roll up our sleeves. It is the task during which we dirty our hands. It is the task of loving not just the people it suits us to love, but loving the unlovable.

Our loving is a response to the loving we have absorbed. 'We love, because he first loved us' (I John 4.19).

. . . I love, but O the whole
Of love is but my answer, Lord, to Thee;
For Thou wast long beforehand with my soul,
Alway Thou lovedst me.

Being loved and loving, being loved and loving, being loved and loving. They go together, hand in hand, throughout life.

❧

The television series I have been watching took us to a very low point tonight. The series has been about a theological college and about some of the students being trained at it for the professional ministry. Well, tonight they met with the students of another theological college and belonging to another denomination. So students A met with students B at the theological college of students B. Students B invited students A to their eucharist. Students A went to it but were not allowed to receive communion.

That was no surprise to students A, and no great surprise to the professionals like myself watching the programme. I wonder, however, what some non-professionals or fringe Christians or outsiders – or Samaritans – thought. Who knows, they might just have guffawed and said 'I told you so – that's what Christianity is like through and through.' But for me it was a chilling moment.

The chilling thought for us professionals, the chilling thought for us pious priests and Levites is that we may have become so preoccupied with observing our religious law (in this case, ecumenical or eucharistic law or whatever) that we may in fact be breaking the law of God, which requires us to love God and love neighbour. The chilling thought is that a Samaritan may know more about observing the law of God than we do.

There's a point at which the whole religious thing simply breaks down and becomes absurd. There's a point at which we have to say that religion has slipped from its moorings, a point at which we have to say that it is doing more harm than good. Religion can become such a tyrant, it can become such a preoccupation, it can become so wound up on itself, it can become more and more concentratedly religious, it can become more and more tightly coiled – that it ceases to be Christian.

It seems to be a feature of prayers of thanksgiving that they begin with thanksgiving, then, after the halfway mark, they switch to an offering of self to the one who is being thanked.

Two things that are at the very heart of discipleship: thanksgiving for what one has received, and a giving of oneself.

> Almighty God, you have showered upon us such an abundance of gifts that we are wonderfully blessed: help us to show our thankfulness to you by dedicating our lives to your service; through Jesus Christ our Lord.

It is unthinkable that we can go through life praying

> *thy kingdom come;*
> *thy will be done*

without actually doing something – doing something rather more than we are doing at present – to achieve the coming of God's kingdom, the doing of God's will.

∽

The central character in Bryce Courtenay's novel *The Power of One* is Peekay, a young white South African of English descent. The novel is a story about relations between English-speaking and Afrikaans-speaking whites and between whites and blacks in the South African apartheid society, a story about Peekay pursuing the ideal of the brotherhood of all people, a story about Peekay swimming against the tide in the midst of South Africa's tensions and hatreds and brutalities. In his battle to maintain his integrity and in his determination to prevail, no matter how great the odds are that are stacked against him, he becomes used to thinking and acting differently from the people around him. This is something his old friend Doc has taught him. He reflects:

> *Doc had taught me the value of being the odd man out. The man assumes the role of the loner, the thinker and the searching spirit who calls the privileged and the powerful to task. The power of one was the courage to remain separate, to think through to the truth and not to be beguiled by*

*convention or the plausible arguments of those
who expect to maintain power, whatever the cost.*

The people who are going to be part of the renaissance of
discipleship will perhaps have to have something of
Peekay's power within them.

∾

As we follow Jesus of Nazareth we are surely led out of
our preoccupation with ourselves and our petty concerns,
and led to become more involved in what concerns him.

I am not, however, wanting people to become activists,
to be active here and there and everywhere, to be doing
this and that and the other. It is not so much a question of
what we *do* as of what we *are*, and then what we do will
flow from what we are.

∾

*Mary said, 'I am the Lord's servant, and I am will-
ing to do whatever he wants.'*

Thus says Mary in the story of the Annunciation.

There is all the difference in the world between Mary's
approach and what is very often our own pernicious
approach. So often we decide what we want to do, and
then we ask for God's blessing on what we have decided
we want to do, and then we do what we have decided we
want to do. The process of asking for God's blessing on
our decision ('offering our decision to him', as some
people put it) somehow makes our doing respectable,

84

acceptable, 'religious'. But that does not undo the fact that we'll have gone about it in an entirely erroneous, contrary manner.

∾

In Irwin's Shaw's novel *The Young Lions* Noah Ackerman is doing his military training in a small town during the Second World War. When he gets some leave, his wife joins him in the town and they begin to spend a week together in a rooming house.

Soon, however, the landlady orders them out because she realizes that Noah is Jewish.

They pack their bags and walk away from the house . . .

> *The landlady was on the porch, still in her grey apron. She said nothing when Noah paid her, merely standing there in her smell of sweat, age and dishwater, looking with silent, harsh righteousness at the soldier and the young girl who walked slowly up the quiet street towards the bus station.*

Righteousness? What a way to travesty a great word! The landlady believes that her way of life is righteous, and yet what she needs urgently is to emerge from her supposed righteousness, she needs to emerge from her self-righteousness. She needs to emerge from her way of life, from her culture, from her prejudices, from herself. She needs to emerge to a righteousness derived from beyond her, derived from beyond her miserable culture, from beyond her miserable self – or derived from depths within herself which she has never before plumbed, derived from depths within herself which she may never even have glimpsed.

❧

The Mountain is not merely something externally sublime. It has a great historical and spiritual meaning for us . . . From it came the Law, from it came the Gospel in the Sermon on the Mount. We may truly say that the highest religion is the Religion of the Mountain. What is that Religion? When we reach the mountain summits we leave behind us all the things that weigh heavily below on our body and our spirit. We leave behind all sense of weakness and depression; we feel a new freedom, a great exhilaration, an exaltation of the body no less than of the spirit. We feel a great joy.

The Religion of the Mountain is in reality the religion of joy, of the release of the soul from the things that weigh it down and fill it with a sense of weariness, sorrow and defeat . . .

Not only on the mountain summits of life, not only on the heights of success and achievement, but down in the deep valleys of drudgery, of anxiety and defeat, we must cultivate this great spirit of joyous freedom and uplift of the soul.

We must practise the religion of the mountain down in the valleys also.

Jan Smuts

❧

As I get older I find myself becoming more and more committed to a notion of Christian discipleship that is more loosely tied to ceremonial, ecclesiastical religion – to the maintenance of services and hierarchies and organs and buildings and so on – and freer to explore the spiritual potential of the human being – our search for meaning, our discovery of who we are, our discovery of how we can lead fuller lives, and so on.

I think there is a difference between the two words, 'religious' and 'spiritual'. I think religion has often hijacked the search for truth on the slopes of the huge hill, therefore I have recently begun to use the word 'religion' in a slightly pejorative sense, and to use the word 'spiritual' to describe the range of the human quest.

One of my favourite collects contains within it the petition 'increase in us true religion'. Part of our quest is a quest for true religion. Perhaps, perhaps, perhaps true religion is a discipleship that is not as dependent on religion as it has generally been.

∽

My relatives and my friends all joined in expostulating with me on the folly of my enterprise. I was a man, they said, who was burying the talent entrusted to him and wanted to trade with false currency. Work among savages I ought to leave to those who would not thereby be compelled to leave gifts and acquirements in science and art unused . . . A lady who was filled with the modern spirit proved to me that I could do much more by

87

*lecturing on behalf of medical help for natives than
I could by the action I contemplated.*

Albert Schweitzer

Schweitzer is describing the reaction he received when it
became known that he had resolved to be a jungle doctor.

I had had something of a debate within myself regard-
ing the wisdom of driving all the way to Weymouth
Hospital to see M. 'It's sheer folly,' one half of me said to
the other half. 'It's sheer folly to drive to Weymouth to see
someone, no matter how dear she may be, who is unlikely
to be able to recognize you – or if able to recognize you,
only dimly. She is too frail, too debilitated. Don't go.
You'll be wasting your time.'

But I did go. I drove all that way to see her *because*, I
suppose, it was sheer folly to do so. I recognized that,
though it was sheer folly to the world, it was perhaps very
much part of divine wisdom for me to go to see her. People
who are compos mentis have a hospital chaplain to relate
to, but a poor frail creature like M. needed me to waste my
time, so to speak, in driving to see her.

While I was on my way I thought of Albert Schweitzer's
words: what his relatives and friends said about the folly
of *his* enterprise. And I was glad I had decided to go.

ω

In a sense I have arrived when I discover myself to be
embraced by a father, clothed with the robe of a son, with
a ring on my hand and shoes on my feet, and the fatted
calf killed for a feast.

And yet I haven't arrived. I am still getting there, growing into the fullness of my sonship. There is still a lifetime ahead of me in which to enjoy the embrace of the father, a lifetime ahead of me in which to contribute to the well-being of his estate.

We must beware of saying 'We know this' or 'We understand that.' We must never say it with any kind of finality or arrogance, because we may find that no sooner have we said it than we receive such a new surge of knowledge or understanding that it seems that formerly we knew or understood not a thing. Always there must be the expectation of further knowledge, further understanding, further growth, further development, further maturity as human beings.

I like very much the prayer of St Richard of Chichester in which there is this petition. The italics are mine.

> May I know thee *more* clearly,
> Love thee *more* dearly,
> And follow thee *more* nearly:
> For ever and ever.

I don't think it is ever a question of merely getting to know him, of merely getting to love him, of merely getting to follow him. The getting to know him and love him and follow him – that is a lifelong affair, ever-unfolding, ever-progressing, ever-deepening.

∾

For what does it profit a man, to gain the whole world and forfeit his life? (Mark 8.36)

Those words came to mind today while I was listening to L (a high-flying friend) telling me something about the flip side of being an executive in business in London: the ruthlessness of big business (or some big business); the inhumanity of it; the long hours demanded by the company from its executives, with little concern shown for the consequences to family life; the cut-throat competition; the trauma he witnesses when the company forecloses on some enticing credit facility it has allowed some individual or family; and so on.

Living as I do in the relatively relaxed atmosphere of West Dorset my response to what he was telling me was fairly predictable. How can people continue to exist like that, I asked. Surely something eventually has to yield to the pressure, something has to give. What gives will be the executive's heart, or his mental health, or his marriage, or . . .

I quoted to my friend the words from St Mark's Gospel.

In Janet Lynch-Watson's biography of the Indian sadhu, Sundar Singh, there are some interesting pages about Sundar Singh's visits to the West in the 1920s. He expressed a disenchantment with the West's preoccupation with materialistic values. He was critical of the bustle and urgency of life in the West: the 'busyness', he said, was inimical to man's spiritual life. He was critical of Western Christianity, saying that the Christians of the West had for too long set too little store by the spiritual dimension. The Christian West possesses the Gospel pearl, but it has been almost lost amidst the heap of accumulations made by theology, church, and culture.

In her postscript Lynch-Watson quotes some beautiful words written by Evelyn Underhill which could be a kind of commentary on these matters.

> *Have we not lost the wonder and poetry of the forest in our diligent cultivation of the economically valuable trees . . .?*

∽

Rembrandt's drawing 'Satan Showing Christ the Kingdoms of the World' depicts the devil, having taken Jesus up a high mountain, showing him all the kingdoms of the world and the glory of them, and saying to him 'All these I will give you, if you will fall down and worship me.' The drawing is not one of Rembrandt's prettiest pictures. In fact it is quite spooky because the devil is portrayed as a winged skeleton. Therefore one knows as soon as one sees the picture that succumbing to the temptation would have meant death to Jesus – death to his values, death to his ideals, death to the spiritual movement he was about to inaugurate, death to himself. Instead he sent the skeleton-devil packing, and chose life. There on the wilderness mountain-top Jesus had a choice between death and life. He chose life.

We are not strangers to such a choice. It is a choice which the Judaeo-Christian tradition has set before people all down the centuries. The skeleton-devil's way leads to death, God's way to life.

The choice is enunciated in the Book of Deuteronomy. Moses has set before his people the privileges and obligations of their covenant relationship with God, and he goes on to say these words.

> *I call heaven and earth to witness against you this day, that I have set before you life and death, blessing and curse; therefore choose life, that you and your descendants may live, loving the Lord your God, obeying his voice, and cleaving to him . . .*
>
> (30.19f.)

∾

Sometimes some truth or some decision or some choice hits one with such force between the eyes that one cannot disregard it. One goes on thinking about it afterwards, trying to sort its significance out in one's mind.

The day after we arrived in Sydney the Red Arrows performed. They spewed out their red, white and blue smoke in a daring, dazzling display, seen against the incomparable Sydney skyline of bush and skyscrapers and Opera House and Harbour Bridge.

The day we left Sydney we watched Oriana arrive on her maiden voyage around the world. We watched her enter the harbour between the Heads and then, accompanied by a cavalcade of motorboats and tugs and sprayed by ceremonial jets of water, move slowly through the harbour to her mooring near the Opera House and Harbour Bridge.

In each case we were confronted by amazing, almost superhuman constructions: the Red Arrows, Oriana, and no less amazing the Sydney skyscrapers and Opera House and Harbour Bridge.

During the flight back to Heathrow it suddenly became crystal-clear to me that somewhere in all this was written a choice on a massive, gargantuan scale. Were these structures part of mankind's idolatry, part of mankind's hankering after self-glory, part of death; or were they part of life, part of mankind's creative collaboration with God, part of mankind's attempt to give glory to God? Of course such a meditation can happen not just on a Boeing 747 flying home from Sydney (and it is hardly fair on Sydney to focus thus on it) but anywhere in our own country, in city or town or village or church. We have a choice before us between the gods and God, between self-glory and giving glory to God, between death and life. It is not just some massive choice centred on huge structures thousands of miles away, but a choice that is with each one of us daily, in one way or another, to a greater or lesser extent.

～

There are, I hope, two threads running through these pages: a concern for the microcosm, the person, the human being, myself, my self; and a concern for the macrocosm, society, the nation, the world.

We see both concerns in the lives of men like John Wesley and William Wilberforce.

We think of Wesley particularly with regard to the regeneration of the individual, but he also had a great social concern: a concern for the poverty and insanitary conditions and disease he encountered on his travels, and also the evidence he saw of the prosperity gained on the back of the slave trade – all of which needed to be remedied.

We think of Wilberforce particularly with regard to the abolition of the slave trade, but he had roots in the piety of the Clapham Sect.

In both men the two concerns – a desire to see the individual renewed and a desire to see society renewed – went inseparably hand in hand.

Most of us live lives that are so limited, so confined. More is required of us: that we should be less self-centred, more open to the need that is evident all around us. And yet there is a limit to how much we can be cajoled into living more expansively, because we simply don't possess the inner resources that will produce that expansiveness.

You can go on flogging a donkey or a pack-horse, but he can't go on carrying his load or he can't walk faster or whatever it is you are requiring of him, because he's worn out, he's run out of steam. The capacity to go on is no longer there. He needs some tender loving care. He needs feeding and watering. His capacity to go on carrying a load is dependent on becoming happier and healthier, it is dependent on his inner well-being.

And so with us. Our doing is external, and the external doing is dependent on our inner being, our inner well-being, and flows from it. The inner being, the inner spirituality – whatever one wishes to call it – winds up the spring that produces the exterior momentum. Therefore discipleship is not so much about what happens on the surface of the disciple as about what happens deep within him.

For example, St Francis of Assisi's sermon to the birds: 'My sisters the birds, you owe so much to God your creator that you must always and everywhere sing his praises . . .' That sublime sermon was not plucked out of thin air – it was a manifestation of the saint's interior philosophy and spirituality: the way Francis saw God as Father, and all his fellow-creatures as brothers and sisters.

What is of primary importance is not the speaking or the doing of discipleship but the inner being.

∾

More or less any fool can be a vicar, acting as a functionary, taking funerals and weddings, presiding over any amount of institutional formalism and legalism and moralism, often pursuing the shabby compromises expected of him. But the work of a priest – ah, the work of a priest is different. That goes much deeper. That is concerned with interior religion, with the transactions between God and people at a much deeper level.

A priest knows that the grief seen at a funeral is surface grief. Real grief occurs when the sun is set and the traffic has stopped, the doors are locked and the lights switched off, and solitariness replaces the companionship of relatives and friends. It occurs in the lonely depths of the soul.

A priest knows that the eucharist is not just a feeding on bread and wine, but a feeding on the grace of Jesus of Nazareth in one's heart.

A priest knows that forgiveness is not just lip forgiveness, but involves forgiving people from one's heart.

A priest knows that adultery is more than the superficial

act. He knows that everyone who looks at a woman lustfully has already committed adultery with her in his heart.

A priest knows that the way to honour God is not just with one's lips but at the level of the heart.

A vicar administers baptism as part of his duty. Perhaps, however, a priest knows in his heart that 'Baptism is nothing; unbaptism is nothing; the only thing that counts is new creation . . . Baptism or unbaptism is neither here nor there; what matters is to keep God's commands.'

∽

As I *remember* Jesus of Nazareth at the eucharist he meets me deep within.

It does not always happen like that. If, for example, I go to the eucharist in my best clothes, intending to impress, if I go pretending, if I go in any of the masks I customarily wear, he will not be able to meet me, the real me, my real self. Therefore I'll walk out of the service as unwhole as when I walked in.

Receiving communion is something that happens inwardly. The bread and wine are the outward and visible sign of an inward and spiritual gift. So often we focus on the outward and visible, forgetting that what it is really about is the inward and spiritual. The eucharist is not about feeding on the outward and visible but about receiving the inward and spiritual.

As I pray 'Almighty God, unto whom all hearts be open' I can have my heart tight shut and locked.

As I pray 'Almighty God, from whom no secrets are hid' I can have secret upon secret hidden away in sealed coffers.

There is no point in my going to the eucharist unless I do away with pretence – as far as I am able to – and give the inward meeting a chance to take place. No amount of churchianity or formalism will contribute to my wholeness.

What I need is for some holy man or story or sudden insight to put a finger on what is, deep down within me, part of the universal human flaw: my self-centredness, the me at the centre of my self, the me saying 'I want this, gimme that.' I can dress those words up so that they sound more elegant and sophisticated, but that is what they mean: 'I want this, gimme that,' indicating a life revolving around myself, me living for myself.

Nothing less than healing deep down will do. Politics can help, and so can education, and so can religion, but what is needed is a spirituality that will go down deeper and touch my stony-hard heart of self-centredness. What I need is for the Old Testament words to become true in me:

Thus says the Lord God: 'A new heart I will give you, and a new spirit I will put within you; and I will take out of your flesh the heart of stone and give you a heart of flesh. And I will put my spirit within you, and cause you to walk in my statutes and be careful to observe my ordinances.'

(Ezek. 36.26f.)

Jesus said to him, 'You shall love the Lord your God with all your heart, and with all your soul, and with all your mind. This is the great and first commandment. And a second is like it, You shall love your neighbour as yourself.'   (Matt. 22.37f.)

Oh heck, that sounds like just another 'Thou shalt' or 'Thou shalt not'. We ministers are so quick to dish up 'Thou shalts' and 'Thou shalt nots'. More religious law, another set of rules, more obligation, more duty, more external law imposed from the outside. And for the most part people are unable to do much about it. And so the guilt piles up.

What we need is for the law of God to be put within us, to be written upon our hearts. Then the law will not just be external to us, imposed from the outside. It will have been internalized. And in becoming internalized it will have ceased to be law. Loving will then be something we do not because we have been told to do it, not because we are 'obedient'. We will do it because it will have become second nature to us, like breathing out and breathing in.

So we must let love be put within us, we must let love be written upon our hearts. The Old Testament words must become true in us:

The Lord says: 'I will put my law within them, and I will write it upon their hearts; and I will be their God, and they shall be my people.'   (Jer. 31.33)

What is a real Christian?

Some people might reply in terms of Christianity's outward and visible requirements, for example the requirement to be baptized.

While not necessarily disagreeing with such a reply I should prefer the inwardness and spiritualness of being a Christian to be emphasized. Therefore my reply might begin something like this:

> He is not a real Christian who is one outwardly, nor is true baptism something external and physical. He is a Christian who is one inwardly, and real baptism is a matter of the heart, spiritual and not literal . . .

❧

After preparing for the early service this morning I made my way down to Church Beach. It was particularly lovely, and I found myself singing with Louis Armstrong 'What a wonderful world'. Then I sat on a rock, and in the silence I felt a gentle companionship with all around me: the beach, the sea, the seagulls on it, the cliffs beyond. I recalled some words given to me yesterday:

> *To be a saint is not to be a solitary lover. It is to enter into deeper community with everyone and everything that exists.*

I was glimpsing the saint's insight. This was where I wanted to belong, this was where I wanted to remain, and yet within minutes I'd have to be back in the Parish

99

Church. It should be the church's task, I reflected, to proclaim a truth like the one I had been glimpsing, but I feared that the limitlessness of my companionship with the natural world would be squeezed to pulp within the confines of the institutional things awaiting me. Within minutes my wings would be clipped.

꩜

How fortunate we are in Lyme to have the beaches, and to have all our other wilderness areas: the Spittles, Ware Cliffs, the Undercliff. How fortunate is anyone anywhere who lives with a stretch of wilderness on his doorstep.

I for one could never live amidst the noise and atmospheric pollution of a built-up area, and I think it is vitally important that people who do live under such conditions should have some means of escape. Therefore I am looking forward to Geoff Hamilton's posthumous gardening series *Paradise Gardens* in which he will demonstrate how gardens can be grown on postage stamps, on little patches of ground at the back of the house, on balconies, such gardens becoming oases in the midst of the desolation of noise and fumes.

꩜

When I stand on Church Beach, filled with wonder, I sometimes believe that I am glimpsing momentarily a tiny piece of the Garden of Eden. I have found my way there through following Jesus of Nazareth, I am there by virtue of having discovered my sonship. For a moment, unfortunately for only a moment, I enjoy a companionship with the natural world, I enjoy a deep communion with everyone and everything that exists.

It is a glimpse of the harmony there should be between man and nature, it is a glimpse of what man is meant to be, it is a glimpse of man's task: to rule over – to be in charge of – the fish of the sea and the birds of the air and every living thing that moves upon the earth. It is a glimpse of the goodness of creation. Behold, it is very good.

From such a glimpse arises a sense of responsibility: a responsibility to work with nature instead of fighting it with unnatural means; to respect nature instead of bisecting it and putting it on display in glass cases for public gaze.

When I die I should like my remains to be buried in unconsecrated ground, as a witness to my belief that ground – plain ground, ordinary ground, unconsecrated ground – is very good. I like the idea of my dead self lying in ordinary ground, there being no need for the church to improve the ground or change it in any way by consecrating it. Being buried in unconsecrated ground would be a final uncompromising attempt to find harmony with the natural world and of course with the God of the natural world.

I don't think I'm naive about nature, I don't think I have any illusions about the natural world being innocuous, nor any romantic notions about wild animals being as cuddly as teddy bears. Who could watch even half a wildlife programme on television without becoming aware of the violence that is needed in the animal kingdom in order to survive? Nature is indeed red in tooth and claw.

Such redness is also part of man's primaeval makeup, but man cannot be left at that primaeval level. Man does not throw in his lot with the animal kingdom at that level, accepting that he is just another savage animal. He has to discover that his status is altogether more exalted, he has to discover his responsibility to be in charge of the animal kingdom. That puts him on an altogether different plane. He has to be in touch with his primaeval redness, yes, but being aware of it he has to aspire to something higher, he has to rise above it, he has to discover that he is at the pinnacle of the animal kingdom. Very much more is required of him than the behaviour of an animal.

❧

In Jesus of Nazareth we reach . . . that rock of love
on which the whole universe is constructed.

The universe built on a rock of love is meant to function according to love.

Woe to anyone introducing into the universe any philosophy or law or behaviour contrary to love.

Man being in charge of the animal kingdom means man loving the animal kingdom.

❧

For St Francis of Assisi God wasn't just his Father but the Father of all.

He saw God as the Father of the wolf who was such a threat to the people of the time; as the Father of water – rainwater, the water in rivers and lakes, the water he washed himself in, the water he drank. He saw God as the Father of the sun he enjoyed during the hot Italian days; as the Father of the moon he loved to look at by night.

The wolf became Brother wolf, water became Sister water, the sun Brother sun, the moon Sister moon.

If we were to adopt this way of thinking it would mean adopting a new way of living. It would mean treating everything in the universe as a brother or sister.

This is one of the ways in which St Francis is making his presence felt among us today. He is urging us to treat the rainforest as Brother rainforest, to treat the whale as Sister whale, the ozone layer as Sister ozone layer.

∾

Living in harmony with the natural world sometimes means having to accept the discomfort that is part of the natural world. The discomfort is inevitably part of how things are, inevitably part of the givenness of life.

For example we are quick to appreciate warm (but not too warm) and sunny (but not too sunny) days, but if the weather is not to our fancy we are quick to complain.

When one walks through the town a lot, as I do, something one learns is that some comment about the weather is a form of human greeting. Therefore instead of 'Good morning' or 'Have a nice day' there will be some remark about the weather.

On a lovely morning the greeting will tend to be 'Fine day, Vicar' or 'Another lovely day, Vicar' or 'Fine summer we're having, Vicar.' So far so good. What I wonder about sometimes is the adverse comment. There comes a misty, rainy day, and the greeting tends to become 'Not very nice today, Vicar' or 'We could do with some good weather, Vicar.'

If I were 100% honest I'd stop in my tracks and challenge what has been said. Instead of selling my soul to the devil by replying 'Yes, a rotten day' and passing on, I'd stop in my tracks and deliver a thirty-second sermon. I'd say 'This is a rainy, misty day, true – but the hydrangeas are grateful for the mist and rain, therefore I think we should be grateful also. Instead of saying "Not very nice today" we should be saying "It's a really fine hydrangea day, a really fine day!".'

∿

We tend to have even less enthusiasm for stormy days – the sort of days that whip up the sea – than we have for rainy, misty days.

I understand that the sea needs the periodic agitation that is given to it by a storm; from time to time it needs to be whipped up. Storms produce bubbles in the sea which cause dissolved organic molecules to coalesce, and such aggregates of such molecules become a source of food for little creatures in the sea. Stormy seas are therefore part of the biological, ecological balance, and we have to accept the discomfort of the stormy days which produce stormy seas.

I also understand only too well – one can hardly be the vicar of a seaside town and not understand this – that stormy seas cause loss of life, loss of human life. Mrs H. who tragically lost her teenage son to a stormy sea will know how over the years I have grieved with her, but my grief does not alter the fact that the biological, ecological nature of a storm fills me with wonder. It is part of the natural world, part of how things are, part of the givenness of life. It is part of the risk taken by human beings whenever they venture outside their front doors.

∾

There are many people trying to breathe new life into the old structures, trying to jolly the churches along. There are many cheerleaders doing their best.

I am not sure they will succeed in the long run. On the contrary, I think that a lot of what we know and may hold dear will have to die.

A lean period is ahead: a depression, a trough, a ditch. But it will not be a sterile hole: it will be a seedbed from which the church of the future will grow.

During that time the kernel of the Christian faith will be guarded by a relatively few people for years, perhaps for a century or more. A candlelight of discipleship will live on, and out of it will grow the new form of the Christian faith, the new form of the Christian presence.

This is not a pessimistic view of the church's future. It is a realistic view, and also a profoundly optimistic view concerning death and resurrection.

The resurrection will come in a way that will be meaningful for people living in perhaps the twenty-second or twenty-third century.

∾

What will the institutional church be like when it emerges from the seedbed?

How can one say? In any case it would be wrong to try to say, it would be wrong to appear to be trying to manipulate the resurrection.

All one can say is that the church will be unimaginably different from what it is like today. Within the seedbed, something new will be produced. The emerging church will be as different from our present churches as, for example, post-Exilic Judaism was from pre-Exilic Judaism; as different from our present churches as the early church after the mission to the Gentiles was from the early church before the mission to the Gentiles; as different from our present churches as the post-Reformation churches were from the pre-Reformation church. And so on.

What comes out of the seedbed will be the product of death and resurrection.

Let's not try to hold back the unholdbackable tide. Let's try to go with it.

∾

In a small French village during the Second World War, there was a marble statue of Jesus with his hands outstretched standing in the courtyard of a quaint little church.

One day a bomb struck too close and the statue was dismembered.

After the battle was over and the enemy had passed through, the citizens of the village decided to find the pieces of their beloved statue and reconstruct it. It was no work of art by Michelangelo or

106

Bernini, but it was part of their lives and they loved it. They gathered the broken pieces and reassembled it. To them the scars on the body added to the statue's beauty.

There was, however, one problem: they were unable to find the hands.

'A Christ without hands is no Christ at all,' someone lamented. 'Hands with scars, yes – but what is a Christ without hands? We need a new statue.'

Then someone else came along with a new idea, and this one prevailed. So today a brass plaque fixed to the statue confronts everyone who looks at it: 'I have no hands but YOUR hands.'

Author unknown

∽

I have no higher vision of the Church than as the Servant of the World, not withdrawn but participating, not embattled but battling, not condemning but healing the wounds of the hurt and the lost and the lonely, not preoccupied with its survival or its observances or its Articles, but with the needs of mankind.

Alan Paton

∽

Each of us embodies a facet of the Servant, participating in the world, battling in the world, healing the wounds of the hurt and the lost and the lonely, occupied with meeting the needs of mankind.

Each of us is a servant embodying a facet of the servantness of Jesus of Nazareth, appointed to preach good news to the poor; sent to heal the brokenhearted and to announce that captives shall be released and the blind shall see, that the downtrodden shall be freed from their oppressors, and that God is ready to give blessings to all who come to him.

∾

The Master and Lord took a towel and a basin of water and stooped to wash his disciples' feet. It was the act of a servant. It was the Master and Lord defining how to be Master and Lord.

That shows mankind how to exercise its mastery over the fish of the sea and over the birds of the air and over every living thing that moves upon the earth. The way for us to be masters over the rest of creation is by being its servants.

∾

We cannot go on serving ad infinitum without refreshment. From time to time we have to let ourselves be served by others, be served by our Master and Lord, by our Master and Lord incognito. We need to be refreshed by being served, before we can go on again to serve others.

It requires humility to be a servant, but it can require even greater humility to submit to being served.

Yet that is the way in which the world is meant to turn, with this to-ing and fro-ing, this endless oscillation between serving and being served.

∾

In so far as the church is a servant of the world it will be giving its back to the smiters, and its cheeks to those who pull out the beard; and it will not be hiding its face from shame and spitting.

That was the lot of the body of Jesus of Nazareth in AD 33 – or whatever the date was – as he suffered at the hands of the Jewish Council and the Roman Governor and the soldiers. Similarly his body in the twentieth century will be suffering in one way or another, in so far as it is a servant; and all of us who are part of the body will be bearing a share of the suffering.

All of us, if we are facets of the servantness of our Lord, can expect to be suffering servants.

∾

I ask myself, 'Is the church willing to be a servant, willing to be a suffering servant to the extent of being despised and rejected by men; to the extent of being a church of sorrows, and acquainted with grief?' To what extent is the church willing to be congruous with Jesus of Nazareth? Is the Parish Church willing to find that congruence, that integrity? Are the other churches in Lyme? Is our deanery? Is our diocese? Is our established national church?

To grieve for the suffering, to pray for them, to relieve them out of one's own affluence is something, but not redemption. The redeemers huddle with the homeless under the dark arches where they sleep at night, wear their filthy rags with them, starve with them, sicken of their diseases with them, remembering always that God Himself could only redeem the soul of the penitent thief by bleeding and dying beside him.

Elizabeth Goudge

❧

To what extent am I sharing in the heroic vision of being suffering servants? It worries me that in my comfortable life I am not. If other people ever read these words of mine I hope it will be recalled by some that Sunday after Sunday I have made it clear in my sermons that I have preached first and foremost to myself. In the words that I am typing now, *that* point must not be lost sight of. If it is ever thought that I am pointing a finger at others (which I am not intending to do) it must be realized that not a finger is being pointed without first being pointed at myself. If it is ever thought that I am judging others (and of course it is not part of my job to do that) it must be realized that I am feeling the judgment first and foremost on myself, on my comfortable life, on my questionable values and priorities.

❧

At the still centre of my soul there is the double awareness that I am both a son and a servant. That is the truth I have discovered about myself, the truth I aspire to live out. It is the status given to me – the status of being a son and being a servant.

The two hearts which beat wildly in the Christian are the heart of a son and the heart of a servant. The two hearts beat as one; or perhaps they are not two hearts but the two chambers of a single heart.

❧

Some people, I understand, live in circles where tipping is the norm. I don't know much about tipping, but I am told that it can – I am not saying it always does – go hand in hand with a sense of power. People tip here, there and everywhere, expecting to get their own way, believing that tipping will get them anywhere, believing that tipping will get them anything at any time. All doors, they believe, are open to them.

All doors may be open to them, except one, except the door into the kingdom of God.

If the door of the kingdom of God is to open for us we need to jettison some of our upside up values and acquire from Jesus of Nazareth some of his upside down values: his humility, his foolishness, his powerlessness, his dependence on the Father, his sense that what we need is not luxuries but bread . . .

I enjoy thinking about Jesus in the hills.

We usually read about him down on the plain among the crowds, but sometimes he would escape from the multitude and go up into the hills. Even there the multitude would find him, and he would perceive that they were about to take him by force to make him king or something, and he would have to go further up into the hills to be on his own.

If he is going to be able to face the multitude again he first has to be able to get up into the hills, or on to a beach, or into the desert, or into some other wilderness area. He has to find refreshment, regain his strength, become reunited with the core of his being.

It is a lesson for us to learn from him. We have to follow him up into the hills, then down to the multitude, then up into the hills again.

∾

My main wilderness area is Church Beach, behind and below the Parish Church. That is the place, more than any other, where I know I can become reunited with the core of my being.

Initially my prayer on Church Beach is just 'Abba! Father!', just 'Jesus is Lord . . . Lord, I love you', the Holy Spirit initiating and facilitating the prayer. Then, after standing in the quiet and perhaps repeating those words over and over, I may move on to become full of thanksgiving, or full of confession, or full of the awareness of the needs of others, or full of the awareness of my own need.

∾

As far as I am concerned, it happens or it doesn't happen. Over the years I have learnt that it doesn't (for me) happen at fixed times or even in fixed places. I cannot conjure it up. I cannot control it. When it happens, it happens. When it happens, the wait for it to happen (since the previous time) has always seemed infinitely worthwhile, although the wait is often attended by the dread that it will never happen again. No matter how momentary it is, I cannot go on without it. But I know that I must never try to force it. If I try to force it, it becomes all shrivelled up and unrecognizable.

We must beware of saying to anyone else 'My way is

the way' or 'My way is the only way or the best way.' Each person has to find his or her own way of letting it happen.

∾

If anyone reads these words he will not get much from them about prayer, or rather he will not get much from them about prayer as usually understood: prayer for ten minutes at the start and end of each day, the discipline of 'saying your prayers' at a particular time in a particular place – that sort of thing.

In any case such ideas can very easily push people into unnecessary despair and guilt when they find they cannot achieve what is generally described as 'prayer'. To other people we often appear, by design or by chance, to be stronger and more competent than we really are. Other people may find it helpful if I, a priest for thirty years, admit that I don't know much about prayer and am not afraid to say so. Everyone must find his own way in which to respond to God.

∾

What I believe I am describing in this diary is a spirituality which is offered to the world. It is a spirituality which does not stop at being a spirituality but moves on to become a sleeves-rolled-up task – and the task does not get turned in to bolster any churchiness but is directed towards meeting the needs of the world.

I am describing a son-servant polarity. But of course that is the wrong word. It is not a polarity. My sonship and servantness are not two poles having contrary qualities but rather a unity of being and doing. The being moves on to the doing; the sonship moves on to the servantness.

I am not sure how well this notion fits in with our present churchgoing model, with so much time and human energy turned in on the church: perceiving religion within the circle of the church, having religious notions about worship and ministry and the sacred. I wonder whether the church that will emerge from its death and resurrection will be less clerical and more lay; will be less of a temple kind of church and more of an ark kind of church; will be more mobile; will be less committed to conventional religion and more committed to study and learning and ethics.

More of an ark kind of church? More mobile? Yes, if greater mobility means greater sensitivity to the desert wind. An immobile structure, no matter how splendid, does not easily possess such sensitivity. Possessing all the power and riches of religion, an immobile structure can easily seal itself up against the desert wind, so that the wind has no access to it, and sensitivity to the wind becomes a thing of the past.

Meanwhile all I ask of my church is an Upper Room providing a quietness and a congruity with Jesus of Nazareth. All I ask of my church is the opportunity to *remember* Jesus – the opportunity to return to him in the eucharist, and then to leave the eucharist with a love and a loyalty containing more substance than the morning mist.

ও

I hope I shall, to the end of my days, continue to search for the Truth that stands on a huge hill, craggèd and steep. I hope I shall continue to go about and about in an attempt to reach her.

We beseech thee, O God, the God of truth,
That what we know not of things we ought to know
Thou wilt teach us.

That what we know of truth
Thou wilt keep us therein.

That what we are mistaken in, as men must be,
Thou wilt correct.

That at whatsoever truths we stumble
Thou wilt yet establish us.

And from all things that are false
And from all knowledge that would be hurtful,
Thou wilt evermore deliver us,
Through Jesus Christ our Lord.

Brooke Foss Westcott

Sources and Acknowledgments

The words by John Donne (1571–1631) which inspired the title come from his poem 'Seek True Religion!'.

p. 5   From Albert Schweitzer, *The Quest of the Historical Jesus* (ET 1910), 3rd edn A. & C. Black 1954, reissued SCM Press 1981, p.401.

pp. 6–7   From *A Gift of Light*, a collection of thoughts from Father Andrew selected and edited by Harry C. Griffith, Morehouse-Barlow, n.d., p.113. Father Andrew was the name by which H.E. Hardy (1869–1946) was known.

p. 8   From Albert Schweitzer, *My Life and Thought: An Autobiography*, Allen & Unwin 1931; Guild Books Edition 1957, p. 106.

p. 12   From G.W.H. Lampe, *I Believe*, Skeffington 1960, p.139.

pp. 15–17   Aggrey's story of the Eagle is related in Edwin's Smith's biography of him, *Aggrey of Africa*, SCM Press 1929, pp.136ff.

p. 18   I was given this poem many years ago, but have been unable to find out anything about its origin or its author.

pp. 19–20   The lines from 'The Magpies in Picardy' by T.P. Cameron Wilson (1889–1918) and from 'In Flanders Fields' by John McCrae (1872–1918) are taken from *Poetry of the First World War* selected by Edward Hudson, Wayland 1988; those from 'Sombre the night is' by Isaac Rosenberg (1890–1918) are taken from *Poems of the First World War* edited by Martin Stephen, Everyman 1993.

p. 23   In Stuart Jackman, *The Davidson Affair*, Faber 1966, p. 77.

p. 23   From John A.T. Robinson, *But That I Can't Believe!*, Fontana 1967, pp.27f.

pp. 28–9   From Julian of Norwich, *Revelations of Divine Love*, pp.67f. and 185 in the Penguin 1966 edition.

p. 36	From Fulton Oursler, *Modern Parables*, Cedar Books 1951, p.34.
p. 50	John A.T. Robinson, *But That I Can't Believe!*, Fontana 1967, p.93.
p. 50	*The Promise of His Glory*, Church House Publishing and Mowbray 1991, pp.177, 170, 103, 137, 139.
pp. 53–4	William Tyndale (*c.* 1494–1536), English Bible translator and reformer, was eventually arrested and burned for his activities. Other extracts are taken from the Burial Service (Alternative Services, First Series) and from David Hope's 'Credo' article in *The Times* of 16 March 1996.
p. 56	As reported in an article in the *Church Times* of 24 June 1994.
p. 57	E.W. Barnes in the Foreword to R.D. Richardson, *The Gospel of Modernism*, Skeffington, n.d. (probably early 1930s), p. 17.
p. 66	John Mason (*c.*1645–94), the last lines of the hymn beginning *How shall I sing that Majesty	Which Angels do admire?*
p. 68	William Shakespeare, *Hamlet*, I.v.
p. 69	William Blake (1757–1827), from 'Auguries of Innocence'.
pp. 70–1	Francis Thompson (1859–1907).
p. 74	The Alternative Service Book 1980, collect for Easter Day.
p. 74	Quoted by Carlo Carretto in *I, Francis*, Fount 1983.
p. 75	The sermon 'Learning from Cancer' was preached in the Chapel of Trinity College on 23 October 1983 and is quoted in full by Robinson's biographer Eric James in his *A Life of Bishop John A.T. Robinson*, Collins 1987, pp. 304ff.
p. 76	The American pastor and theologian Walter Rauschenbusch (1836–1918) was the father of the social gospel in the United States in the early part of this century. His most enduring work is *A Theology for the Social Gospel*, which was reissued in 1997 by Westminster John Knox Press, Louisville. I do not know the source of this poem of his, but it is quoted by George Appleton in *Journey for a Soul*, Fontana 1974, pp.225f.
p. 76	The Alternative Service Book 1980, collect for Pentecost 14.
p. 77	John 17.3 in the Revised English Bible version.

p. 77	Written in 1914. The unknown author was killed in 1917.
p. 77	In Stuart Jackman, *The Davidson Affair*, Faber 1966, p.74.
p. 81	The author of these four lines is unknown to me.
p. 82	The prayer is my own.
pp. 83–4	Bryce Courtenay, *The Power of One*, Mandarin 1989, p.442.
p. 84	Luke 1.38 in The Living Bible version.
p. 85	Irwin Shaw, *The Young Lions*, Jonathan Cape 1949; The Reprint Society 1951, pp. 275f.
p. 86	Jan Smuts, from his famous address at the unveiling of the Mountain Club War Memorial on Table Mountain in February 1923; taken from *The Thoughts of General Smuts* compiled by P.B. Blanckenberg, Juta & Co 1951, pp.222f.
pp. 87–8	Albert Schweitzer, *My Life and Thought: An Autobiography*, Allen & Unwin 1931; Guild Books Edition 1957, p.84.
pp. 90–1	Janet Lynch-Watson, *The Saffron Robe*, Hodder 1975, pp.149f. She is quoting from Evelyn Underhill, *The Life of the Spirit and the Life of Today*, Methuen 1922.
p. 96	Top of page: biblical quotations are adapted from Gal. 6.15 and I Cor. 7.19 (REB).
p. 99	Adapted from Rom.2.28f.
p. 99	The words are attributed to K.L. Woodward, but unfortunately I know nothing about him.
p. 102	John A.T. Robinson, *But That I Can't Believe!* Fontana 1967, p.28.
p. 107	Alan Paton, *Instrument of Thy Peace*, Fontana 1969, p.69.
p. 108	Top of page: based on Luke 4.18–19 in the Living Bible version.
pp. 109–10	Elizabeth Goudge, *Saint Francis of Assisi*, Duckworth 1959, p.190.
p. 115	Brooke Foss Westcott (1825–1901) was, with his contemporaries J.B. Lightfoot and F.J.A. Hort, one of the 'Cambridge Triumvirate', all Professors of Divinity: Westcott and Hort were responsible for a famous edition of the Greek text of the NT. Westcott was another Bishop of Durham to show a deep concern for social issues and mediate in a miners' strike. He was the founder of Westcott House.